Boost Your Computational and Complex Thinking – Impulsa tu Pensamiento Computacional y Razonamiento Complejo

Future of Education – Futuro de la Educación

Eds. María Soledad Ramírez-Montoya, Rasikh Tariq, Leonardo David Glasserman Morales,
Edgar Omar López-Caudana & Inés Alvarez-Icaza Longoria

VOL. 3

María Soledad Ramírez-Montoya, Rasikh Tariq, Edgar Omar López-Caudana, José Martín Molina Espinosa, Miguel González Mendoza, Carlos Enrique George-Reyes, Magally Martínez Reyes, Irma Azeneth Patiño Zúñiga, Fidel Antonio Guadalupe Casillas-Múñoz, Hugo Alexander Rozo-García, Paloma Suárez Brito & Pamela Geraldine Olivo Montaño

---

Boost Your Computational and Complex Thinking – Impulsa tu Pensamiento Computacional y Razonamiento Complejo

E4C&CT Digital Ecosystem Platform – Plataforma de Ecosistema Digital E4C&CT

PETER LANG

Berlin · Bruxelles · Chennai · Lausanne · New York · Oxford

Bibliographic Information published by the Deutsche Nationalbibliothek
The Deutsche Nationalbibliothek lists this publication in the Deutsche Nationalbibliografie; detailed bibliographic data is available online at http://dnb.d-nb.de.

Library of Congress Cataloging-in-Publication Data
A CIP catalog record for this book has been applied for at the Library of Congress.

Cover Credit: Michael Haderer, Vienna, Austria

ISSN 3053-4593 (Print) | 3053-4607 (Online)
ISBN 978-3-631-93303-9 (Print)
ISBN 978-3-631-93318-3 (ePDF)
ISBN 978-3-631-93319-0 (ePUB)
DOI 10.3726/b22653

info@peterlang.com

PETER LANG Open

Published by Peter Lang GmbH, Berlin, Germany

This publication has been peer reviewed.

www.peterlang.com

Contact for General Product Safety Regulation (GPSR): gpsr@peterlang.com

Table of Contents

Boost Your Computational and Complex Thinking

E4C&CT Digital Ecosystem Platform

Figure 1.
IRG-R4C Researchers mobilise the E4C&CT Digital Ecosystem platform

About Us

We are members of the IRG-R4C Interdisciplinary Research Group Scaling Complex Thinking for All (Figure 1). We are passionate about taking higher education to new levels of excellence. We are dedicated to developing and promoting advanced reasoning competencies to face the complexity of the modern world. We use open science strategies and the most advanced 5.0 technologies, such as artificial intelligence and data science, to create training systems that prepare people for the challenges of the future. Our work is linked to projects that integrate universities, industries, the government and the civil sector, always seeking sustainable solutions that benefit the whole society.

Our vision is clear and ambitious: to contribute meaningfully to the future of education, creating innovative solutions to the problems and challenges of today's society. We align with the goals of UNESCO's 2030 Agenda for Sustainable Development, fostering interdisciplinary collaboration and building robust academic networks. At IRG-R4C, we work to train a new generation of highly competitive professionals committed to social welfare who always seek to enable innovative solutions that respond to present and future challenges.

Editorial Letter

Let's visualise a new way of thinking that connects humans with machines: computational thinking. This revolutionary approach allows us to break down complex problems into manageable parts, find patterns and create efficient solutions using logic and systematic reasoning. By adopting computational thinking, we will not only improve our ability to interact with technology, but we will also develop a mindset that empowers us to meet the challenges of the twenty-first century in innovative and effective ways.

Our project develops a digital ecosystem, a platform called E4C&CT, to scale computational thinking, from which real-world scenarios with different levels of complexity are presented. Using artificial intelligence tools, we manage and visualise data, and we apply intelligent analysis processes to study how computer science users solve problems. It's as if we're creating a virtual lab where we can observe, learn and improve our skills together.

Computational thinking isn't just a technical skill; it is a new form of literacy that all people must acquire. In an increasingly technology-driven world, understanding how algorithms work and how we can use them to solve problems gives us a competitive advantage and prepares us for an uncertain but possible future. But the benefits don't end there. Educational institutions and decision-makers also benefit, as the results of our research can guide future educational interventions and respond to the growing market for education and learning analytics. In addition, we plan to collaborate with the world's leading research centres, which means that we will be creating a global community dedicated to improving education and technology.

We invite you to be part of this exciting adventure and to build a future full of innovation and collaboration with us!

OBJECTIVES

Our main goal is to design and evaluate a digital ecosystem that emulates real-world environments. This ecosystem uses tools such as artificial intelligence, machine learning and data science to diagnose, develop, and evaluate computational problem-solving skills in college students. We want to help you improve your ability to think in a complex and computational way, not only for studying but also for the challenges that arise throughout life.

SPECIFIC OBJECTIVES

1. Develop a platform that integrates teaching procedures to understand computational problem-solving with automated tools based on learning analytics, artificial intelligence, gaming, machine learning and data science. These tools allow us to analyse behaviours and improve our complex reasoning skills.

2. Implement and evaluate the digital ecosystem in higher education institutions in Latin America and Spanish-speakers, diagnosing, developing and evaluating students' skills in problem-solving and complex reasoning through quantitative and qualitative methods. In addition, we validate the performance of the ecosystem in terms of technological capabilities and user experience.

3. Register copyright licensing, methodologies, content and knowledge to transfer intellectual property through a startup.

Figure 2.
General and specific objectives of the E4C&CT: Ecosystem for scaling up computational thinking and reasoning for complexity

Objectives

Introduction

Did you know that 65% of people who are currently studying will work in jobs that do not exist yet (Computerworld University, 2016)? In a world where technology is advancing by leaps and bounds, how we teach computational thinking skills is more crucial than ever. Computational thinking is a fundamental skill that involves abstracting problems and formulating solutions that can be automated. The teaching of science, technology, engineering and mathematics is increasingly recognised as essential in an information-based society. It is not only about knowing how to programme computers but also about applying computer methods and techniques to find efficient and logical solutions. For example, it involves breaking down large problems into smaller, more manageable parts, finding patterns and following step-by-step processes.

Computational thinking is an essential skill in the digital age, but many educational programmes still don't address it effectively. This open educational resource aims to fill that gap. To achieve this, an ecosystem that simulates real situations of different complexities has been designed and developed. The objective is to improve people's problem-solving skills. By doing so, we prepare ourselves to face the challenges of the twenty-first century in different areas. Likewise, this resource is distinguished by its innovative approach, in which simulated scenarios are used to teach computational thinking in a practical and effective way. Previous studies (Melro et al., 2023, Su & Yang, 2023) have attempted to address these problems with more theoretical methods, but our practical and contextualised approach promises to be more effective and prepares us to act in different present and future scenarios.

With this motivation, the Digital Ecosystem project arises to scale computational thinking and complex thinking skills and focuses on training people for the future of work in a digital ecosystem that emulates real-world environments in a way that is accessible, inclusive and relevant to the requirements of the current labour market (Figure 3). The project establishes the E4C&CT platform, which is an educational resource that will benefit a wide spectrum of professionals and the general public. In addition, decision-makers in the education sector will be able to use the results of this research to design more effective educational interventions adapted to current needs. This is especially important for students with special needs and those living in disadvantaged contexts, thus ensuring more inclusive and equitable education.

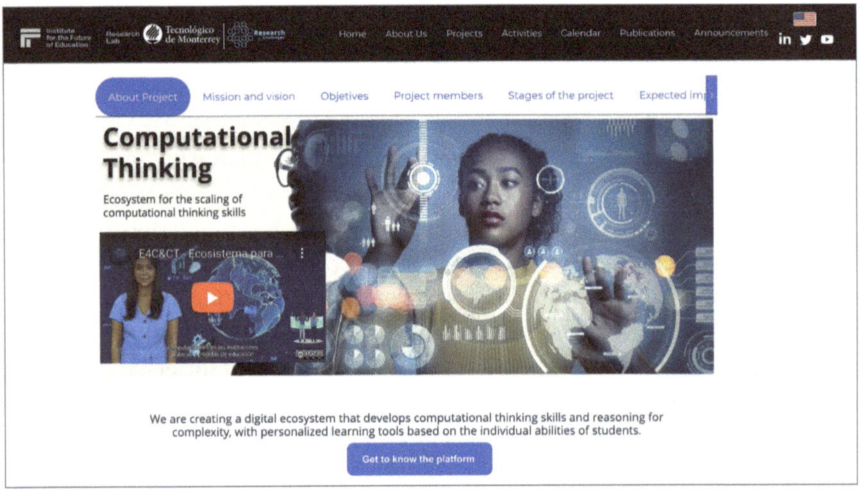

Figure 3. E4C&CT project website (https://www.research4challenges.world/computationalthink)

The E4C&CT platform incorporates scenarios related to several Sustainable Development Goals (SDGs), specifically targeting global issues such as health, water, energy, education and inequalities. This platform uses a computational thinking approach and enhances complex thinking through scenario-based learning. Continuously evolving through artificial intelligence and educational data mining, it offers a unique experience for participants from diverse backgrounds, particularly in Spanish-speaking countries. The platform features a distinctive gamification-inspired instructional design that includes interactive forums, project-based learning and case studies, open educational resources (OER), and educational and instructional videos. This design promotes an engaging learning environment where students can practice skills such as abstraction, pattern identification, decomposition and algorithmic thinking.

As an open access platform with no geographical restrictions, the content offers a complete journey from pre-assessment to post-assessment, leading to multiple project-based learning experiences and culminating in a micro-certificate, all managed within the platform. This material has the potential to redefine the future of education by integrating computational thinking into learning. By continuing to innovate, we can ensure that future generations develop the skills to meet the challenges and opportunities of the digital world. Innovating in education is not an option but a necessity in building a more inclusive and future-proof society.

Despite the increasing emphasis on developing computational thinking (CT) skills across various educational contexts, many current approaches remain overly theoretical, and lack the practical, contextualised frameworks necessary to prepare learners for real-world complexities. Existing platforms and programmes often fall short in integrating real-world scenarios that promote both computational and complex thinking, critical skills for addressing contemporary global challenges. This project seeks to bridge this gap by introducing the E4C&CT Digital Ecosystem, which integrates scenario-based learning with advanced technologies such as artificial intelligence and data science to scale computational thinking skills across diverse disciplines.

What sets the E4C&CT platform apart is its use of simulated real-world scenarios aligned with the United Nations Sustainable Development Goals (SDGs), encouraging learners to engage with global challenges in health, energy, education, and equity. Unlike conventional CT programmes that focus solely on abstract problem-solving techniques, our platform promotes an interdisciplinary approach. This method links CT with complex thinking, equipping learners with the ability to address multifaceted problems through critical analysis, systems thinking, and algorithmic strategies. The E4C&CT platform extends beyond coding and computation, offering a comprehensive, practical learning experience designed to prepare individuals for emerging careers in a rapidly evolving digital landscape.

Furthermore, the platform emphasises accessibility and inclusivity. While many educational resources are geographically or economically restricted, E4C&CT is designed to be open, accessible, and adaptable to diverse learner groups, including those from disadvantaged backgrounds. By incorporating gamification elements and artificial intelligence tools, the platform provides personalised learning experiences, enabling participants to track their progress as they navigate through various stages of complexity. This makes it a highly effective resource for educators and decision-makers, offering valuable insights that can inform future educational interventions and policies.

In conclusion, this project addresses a critical gap by providing an innovative, practical, and scalable solution for fostering both computational and complex thinking skills. It not only prepares individuals for the future workforce but also advances the broader goals of equitable and quality education as outlined by the SDGs. By offering a unique approach to education, the E4C&CT platform is poised to transform how we teach and learn in the digital age, ensuring future generations are equipped to tackle the world's most pressing challenges.

References

Computerworld University (2016). 65 % of the jobs in 2023 still do not exist. Retrieved 24 June 2024, from https://www.computerworlduniversity.es/actualidad/el-65-de-los-trabajos-de-2023-todavia-no-existen

Melro, A., Tarling, G., Fujita, T., & Kleine Staarman, J. (2023). What Else Can Be Learned When Coding? A Configurative Literature Review of Learning Opportunities Through Computational Thinking. Journal of Educational Computing Research, 61(4), 901–924. https://doi.org/10.1177/07356331221133822

Su, J., & Yang, W. (2023). A systematic review of integrating computational thinking in early childhood education. Computers and Education Open, 4, 100122. https://doi.org/10.1016/j.caeo.2023.100122

How is Complex Thinking Linked to Computational Thinking?

Complex thinking is a way of understanding reality in which situations are viewed as an interconnected whole and the mutual influence of multiple factors is recognised. It is not a matter of dividing problems into isolated parts but of considering how all the elements interact with and affect each other. In contrast, computational thinking focuses on breaking down problems into smaller, more manageable steps using logic and algorithms to find efficient solutions.

Combining complex thinking with computational thinking can help us address complex challenges such as those raised in the Sustainable Development Goals, e.g. health, education, inequalities. By marrying complex thinking with computational thinking, we can take a more comprehensive and detailed view of problems and search for alternatives.

The potential of complex thinking is that it allows us to see problems from multiple angles, considering all their variables and relationships. Meanwhile, computational thinking gives us the tools to break down these problems into smaller, more manageable steps using logic and algorithms to find efficient solutions. By bringing these two skills together, we can tackle the most complicated challenges in a more effective, creative and structured way.

Computational thinking complements and enriches complex thinking by offering tools to break down complex problems into more manageable and solvable components, a process known as decomposition. Essentially, this competence encourages the formulation of step-by-step solutions (algorithms), which makes it easier to identify patterns and abstract concepts beyond concrete data. This ability to analyse and synthesise is crucial when facing complex problems in areas such as technology, science and mathematics as it allows us to apply structured and systematic logic. By integrating computational thinking into complex thinking, the ability to anticipate consequences, evaluate multiple possible solutions and apply innovative and efficient approaches to solving real-world problems is enhanced.

TO KNOW MORE ...
About Complex Thinking and Computational Thinking

The Well-Ordered Mind: Rethinking Reform, Reforming Thought

Author: Edgar Morin

Reference: Morin, E. (2020). The well-ordered mind: rethinking reform, reforming thought. XXI century.

▶ This book proposes essential principles for understanding how each part of a problem connects to the whole and vice versa. Morin guides us through a vision that overcomes fragmented knowledge, revealing the invisible interactions between parts and the whole, and addresses essential issues from a holistic perspective. This approach not only enriches our scientific understanding but also unites scientific and humanistic thinking, creating a more complete and reflective view of our human destiny. By reforming our thinking, we can organise knowledge in a way that unites these two traditionally separate cultures. Thus, teaching becomes a process that not only fills our minds but also orders them, teaching us about the human condition, how to live fully, how to face uncertainty and how to be responsible citizens. We invite you to read this book and discover how complex thinking and computational thinking can be integrated to improve both our education and our understanding of the world.

Learning the Components of Computational Thinking Mediated by a Virtual Application of Education 4.0 in the Complex Thinking Environment

Authors: Carlos Enrique George-Reyes, Jessica Alejandra Ruiz-Ramírez, Yessica Betzabe Contreras Fuentes, Edgar Omar López-Caudana

Reference: George-Reyes, C., Contreras, Y., Ruiz-Ramírez, J. & López-Caudana, E. (2023). Learning of the components of computational thinking mediated by a virtual application of education 4.0 in the complex thinking environment. *Educating 59*(2), 1–20. https://doi.org/10.5565/rev/educar.1645 https://hdl.handle.net/11285/650977

▶ This fascinating study presents how Education 4.0 and its applications, such as web-based virtual reality (WebVR), can revolutionise learning. The acceptance of these technologies and the academic performance of 258 students who participated in a knowledge rally designed in a three-dimensional virtual world were evaluated. Through this research, it was shown that simulated reality scenarios not only encourage interaction and the development of communication and collaboration skills but also improve academic performance. The results showed a high acceptance of these virtual environments as learning spaces. However, challenges were also identified, such as the need for computers with high processing capacity and the development of digital skills for both teachers and students.

Open Model of Complex Thinking for the Future of Education

Authors: María Soledad Ramírez-Montoya, Fabián Eduardo Basabe, Martina Carlos Arroyo, Irma Azeneth Patiño Zúñiga, I. A. & May Portuguez Castro.

Reference: Ramírez-Montoya, M. S., Basabe, E., Carlos Arroyo, M., Patiño Zúñiga, I. A., Portuguez Castro, M. (2024). *Open model of complex thinking for the future of education.* Octahedron. https://hdl.handle.net/11285/652033

▶ To discover more about complex thinking, we invite you to explore an innovative educational approach presented in this text. This approach is designed to respond to the demands of the modern world, integrating the various dimensions of thinking – critical, scientific, systemic and innovative. The objective is to train empathetic citizens who are committed to sustainable development. This model is applied not only in academic environments but also in government and business sectors, highlighting the importance of collaboration, empathy and commitment to sustainable solutions to global problems. By immersing yourself in this approach, you will be able to develop skills that will allow you to contribute meaningfully to society and the well-being of the planet.

Educational Innovation in Action

E4C&CT Platform

Education is constantly evolving, adapting to the changing needs of society and the labour market. In this context, the E4C&CT (https://e4cct.mx/) platform emerges as an innovative tool that seeks to develop computational thinking skills through the recognition of the challenges linked to the Sustainable Development Goals (SDGs). This educational platform offers courses specifically designed to foster these essential skills for the twenty-first century. Scan the following QR code to access the platform:

E4C&CT: A Learning Ecosystem

E4C&CT integrates a series of courses focused on different challenges related to the SDGs. Courses include, but are not limited to the following:

- Charting Health. Epidemiology and phylogenetics. This course focuses on understanding public health and disease genetics, promoting research and analysis of epidemiological data.

- EduInnovaTech. Decomposing challenges for quality education. Designed to address challenges in education, this course seeks to improve the quality of education through innovation and technology.
- SolarCT. Computational thinking and energy. A course focused on the use of computational thinking to solve problems related to sustainable energy, this course encourages the creation of innovative solutions for the management and use of energy resources.
- Equality4all. Reducing inequalities by applying complex thinking. This course addresses social and economic inequalities, teaching students how to apply complex thinking to develop inclusive and equitable strategies.

Hands-On Approach and Real-World Experience in E4C&CT Courses

The courses offered at E4C&CT go beyond theory, promoting practice and the application of knowledge in real projects. Students can work in teams, develop prototypes and present their ideas to a panel of experts. This practical approach gives them concrete experience and prepares them to face the challenges of today's world.

Scaling Complex Thinking

Complex thinking is an essential skill for learning about the SDGs. This skill allows people to analyse complicated situations, identify problems and find innovative solutions. At E4C&CT, we focus on developing this type of thinking through challenging activities and exercises. We use case studies, simulations and interdisciplinary projects to teach students how to approach problems from different angles, helping them find comprehensive and effective solutions.

Developing Complex Thinking for the SDGs

E4C&CT courses are designed to inspire students to create initiatives that make a positive impact on their communities and the world. These courses address crucial topics such as public health, quality education, sustainable energy and reducing inequalities, providing students with the necessary tools to design and execute projects that address critical global issues. By completing these courses, students develop computational thinking skills while gaining a deep understanding of how their actions can contribute to the achievement of the SDGs by positively impacting society.

Successful Implementation in the University

As part of its multiple implementations, E4C&CT invited students from Humanities, Engineering, Health, Administration and Economics, as well as High School Teacher Training Schools (EFPEM) in Guatemala, Peru, Panama, Colombia, Chile and Costa Rica to participate in an extracurricular training experience called 'SolarCT: Computational Thinking and Energy'. During 2024, 927 students from the universities participated in this experience, with very positive results: a significant increase in their computational thinking skills and their ability to apply complex thinking in real projects was observed.

E4C&CT represents a major breakthrough in education on the SDGs, offering a dynamic and hands-on learning environment that prepares students for real-world challenges. By combining courses in health, education, energy, and equity with a focus on developing computational and complex thinking skills, this platform is positioned as an indispensable tool for training the next generation of leaders. The implementation at the Universidad San Carlos de Guatemala highlights its effectiveness and potential to transform the educational ecosystem and contribute to the achievement of the SDGs in various contexts.

WHAT DO THE STUDIES SAY?

.... On the Proposal Made by the Innovation Project

We know that we live in a digitalised world, and therefore computational thinking is increasingly necessary and relevant, it is not enough to use the computer, it is increasingly common to develop online activities to learn and to know. An educational platform specifically designed to help us can guide us in the understanding and comprehension of complex problems, make them more manageable and be able to generate patterns of understanding or algorithms to solve them.

Platform where artificial intelligence (AI) is integrated to promote complex thinking in higher education students (Sanabria-Z et al., 2023). The didactic strategy was based on the Transition Design approach, addressing the Collaborative Economy as a challenge. The process of developing AI-supported activities, the challenges and risks identified, as well as a classification model and improvements for future implementations, are detailed in this work. The findings offer a guide for balancing AI-powered educational activities and the development of complex thinking in participants.

The above skills are not unique to careers in technology or computer science, they are applicable in fields as diverse as economics, finance, and energy. Therefore, the opportunity to participate in online activities with the aim of mastering computational thinking will seem challenging at first, but takes us through interactive exercises, games or even challenges that adapt to various levels of ability, therefore, not only theoretical knowledge, but those also that with practice help us in the solution of real and complex problems.

The platform should allow students to learn gradually, at their own pace and from anywhere with internet access. In the university and educational context in general, it is crucial that students develop a problem-oriented mindset and a greater ability to face the challenges of the twenty-first century.

Reference

Sanabria-Z, J., Alfaro-Ponce, B., Argüelles-Cruz, A., & Ramírez-Montoya, M. S. (2023). AI-Based Platform Design for Complex Thinking Assessment: A Case Study of an Ideathon Using the Transition Design Approach. Computers in the Schools, 40(4), 391–411. https://doi.org/10.1080/07380569.2023.2256711

WE INVITE YOU TO REFLECT …

How do you think computational thinking can influence the way we approach and solve problems in our daily lives? In what way do you think they are related?

___

___

___

You've probably heard the phrase 'we live in a digitalised world.' In that context, how do you think the development of skills in computational thinking can offer you a competitive advantage in the labour market or in any other scenario in which you participate?

___

___

___

What benefits do you think computational thinking can bring to academic disciplines that are not directly related to computer science?

___

___

___

SDGs in Education

This educational innovation project was conceived in light of the SDGs, specifically SDGs 3, 4, 7 and 10, and focuses on health and well-being, quality education, promoting affordable and non-polluting energy and reducing inequalities (Figure 4). The project aims to offer innovative training experiences that help scale computational thinking, complex thinking in the digital age and other competencies of the twenty-first century.

Figure 4. SDGs mobilised through the E4C&CT Digital Ecosystem platform

The E4C&CT platform is positioned as an open environment that offers innovative training experiences, is accessible in terms of the minimum level of previous computational skills required as well as its availability and digital ergonomics. In addition, it allows the development and certification of computational thinking competencies and is designed to be used by K-12 students, teachers, facilitators in companies, governments, foundations and people interested in lifelong learning. This allows us to train people for the future of work through real-world situations as the platform is accessible, inclusive and relevant to the requirements of the current labour market.

TO KNOW MORE …

The Link between the SDGs and the Proposal

Unlocking Sustainable Development Goals through Computational Thinking: A Search to Inform Computers Education from Citizen Science Dataset

Authors: María Soledad Ramírez-Montoya, Mariana Buenestado Fernández & Gerardo Ibarra Vázquez

Reference: Ramírez-Montoya, M. S., Buenestado-Fernandez, M. & Ibarra-Vazquez, G. (2023). Unlocking Sustainable Development Goals through Computational Thinking: A Search to Inform Computers Education from Citizen Science Dataset. In *2023 The 8th International Conference on Information and Education Innovations* (ICIEI 2023), Manchester, United Kingdom. ACM, New York, NY, USA. https://doi.org/10.1145/3594441.3594449. https://hdl.handle.net/11285/650450

▶ We invite you to discover this fascinating study that links complex thinking with computational thinking, showing how they can boost high-impact problem solving together. This study analysed the relationship between computational thinking and the SDGs using text mining and data visualisation techniques. Through a detailed analysis of text fragments tagged with the SDGs, it was found that computational thinking sub-competencies – decomposition, pattern recognition, abstraction and algorithms – frequently relate to key SDGs, such as quality education, gender equality, clean water and sanitation, and sustainable cities and communities. The results demonstrate how computational thinking can offer innovative solutions to global problems and support the achievement of the SDGs.

Virtual Reality-Based Computational Thinking and Complex Reasoning: Sequential Case Study

Authors: Carlos Enrique George-Reyes, Edgar Omar López-Caudana, María Soledad Ramírez-Montoya & Jessica Alejandra Ruiz-Ramírez

Reference: George-Reyes, C., López-Caudana, E. O., Ramírez-Montoya, M. S., & Ruiz-Ramírez, J. (2023). Virtual reality-based computational thinking and complex reasoning: sequential case study. *NET. Journal of Distance Education 23*(73). http://dx.doi.org/10.6018/red.540841 https://hdl.handle.net/11285/650112

▶ To help you learn more, we share with you a study that links complex thinking with computational thinking (CT), showing how the quality of education can be transformed. In a study on 176 university students, two tools were used to measure the acceptance of the virtual environment and the development of complex reasoning. The results were surprising: students found the Virtual Campus tool easy to use and useful, and the 3D experience significantly improved their scientific and critical thinking competencies. This study demonstrates that the convergence of CT, complex thinking and WebVR can create innovative learning dynamics that are aligned with the demands of ever-evolving education and contribute to improving problem-solving practices.

New Educational Scenarios

The project aims to equip users with problem-solving skills through a practical approach by utilising the E4C&CT platform, which connects educational efforts to broader social challenges presented in the SDGs as simulated scenarios to teach complex problem solving. To this end, the platform proposes potential scenarios of application, presented as general action lines that can be adapted to the cultural, social, economic or professional context of each user, fostering lifelong learning.

EDUCATIONAL SCENARIO aimed at students

Applying computational thinking to reduce inequality in access to education

Linked SDGs

4 QUALITY EDUCATION

Activity

Participants will develop computational thinking skills—especially decomposition—by analyzing unequal access to education in their local context, aligned with SDG 4 (Quality Education). After an initial research phase to identify key economic, geographic, cultural, and gender-related barriers, students create a mind map that breaks the problem into sub-problems and proposes feasible solutions for each, fostering critical and systemic thinking. The activity concludes with a brief reflection, and assessment is conducted through analytical rubrics evaluating problem identification, depth of analysis, organization, and quality of solutions, with the mind map as the main evidence of learning.

Objective

To analyse the complex problem of unequal access to education through the application of decomposition techniques, a sub-competence of computational thinking, to propose solutions that are applicable at the local level.

Beginning

The first step is to conduct initial research to identify the causes of unequal access to education in your local community. It is crucial to consider factors, such as economic, geographical, cultural and gender barriers. This preliminary stage will not only provide you with a clear view of the problem but also prepare you to apply decomposition techniques efficiently. Make sure you gather accurate and relevant information that allows you to address the problem in a comprehensive and informed manner.

Development

Problem identification: Conduct initial research on the causes of unequal access to education in your local community, identifying factors such as economic, geographic, cultural and gender barriers.

Application of the decomposition technique:

a) Build a mind map to subdivide the problem.
b) Identify inequality in access to education at the centre and create branches of possible causes, such as the lack of educational infrastructure in rural areas, gender discrimination, inadequate educational resources and teaching materials and economic inequality among students' families.
c) Add or remove factors based on the situation in your community.
d) For each branch that identifies sub-problems, build sub-branches by placing ideas with possible solutions. For example, for the branch of gender discrimination in access to education, you could place the development of awareness campaigns on the importance of education for all people.
e) Add a possible solution to each sub-problem.

Closing

Have a personal reflection on the process of decomposition and how this approach helped you better understand the problem and propose feasible and applicable solutions to problems in your community. To learn more about computational thinking, we invite you to take the course EduInnovaTech: Decomposing Challenges for Quality Education, which is available at https://e4cct.mx/.

Evaluation

The evaluation will be through analytical rubrics. The evaluation rubric we propose offers an analytical approach to measure performance at each stage of the process. It is organised into five criteria: Identification of the problem, Application of the decomposition technique, Structure and organisation of the mind map, Proposal of solutions, and Creativity and visual clarity. Each criterion is rated on a four-level scale (1 to 4), from 'Needs improvement' to 'Excellent', providing clear descriptions for each level. For example, in problem identification, the highest level is achieved by including multiple relevant factors (economic, cultural, gender, etc.) with specific examples from the community. Similarly, to assess creativity and visual clarity, the mind map is expected to be not only functional, but also attractive, with graphic elements that facilitate understanding. This rubric allows for transparent evaluation, helping both participants and evaluators understand expectations.

Evidence of Learning

The mind map decomposes the problem of unequal access to education into sub-problems, and for each sub-problem, at least one possible solution is identified.

Digital Materials or Tools

The mind map can be created through technological tools or on paper.

EDUCATIONAL SCENARIO aimed at teachers

Workshop on the development of competencies in computational and complex thinking for teachers

Linked SDGs

4 QUALITY EDUCATION

Activity

Participants will develop computational and complex thinking competencies by designing pedagogical strategies to address unequal access to education, aligned with SDG 4 (Quality Education). Through a real-world scenario, teachers apply principles such as decomposition, pattern recognition, and systems analysis to identify key factors and understand the problem at multiple levels. Using collaborative, practice-based activities and tools like concept maps and flow diagrams, they design context-sensitive and scalable solutions. The activity concludes with the co-creation and presentation of proposals with peer feedback, fostering critical reflection, collaborative problem-solving, and the application of computational thinking to pedagogical innovation.

Objective

To train teachers in the use and application of pedagogical strategies to develop computational and complex thinking skills in their students through a scenario of access to education for all.

Beginning

The workshop begins with an introduction to the concept of computational thinking and its relevance in solving complex problems. The problem of unequal access to education is presented, highlighting its global and local impact. Through a short theoretical session, teachers will learn how to break down complex problems into manageable parts, identifying the underlying factors that contribute to educational inequality. This approach will allow participants to better understand the multiple dimensions of the problem, facilitating the development of more effective and targeted solutions.

Development

During the practical phase, teachers will work in groups to apply decomposition techniques to the problem of unequal access to education. They will be guided in identifying and breaking down the components of the problem, including economic, social and geographic barriers, that affect access to education in their communities. Using concept maps and flowcharts, teachers will organise and analyse the information collected, allowing them to clearly visualise the interrelationships and critical points that need to be addressed.

Closing

The groups will work together to generate locally applicable solution proposals. These proposals will be discussed and refined collectively, encouraging the exchange of ideas and experiences. At the end of the workshop, each group will present their analysis and proposed solutions, receiving feedback from both their peers and facilitators.

Evaluation

The evaluation of the activity will be carried out through analytical rubrics that will measure the performance of teachers in several dimensions, such as the identification of key concepts, understanding and application of computational thinking, the ability to decompose complex problems and the effectiveness of the proposed solutions.

Evidence of Learning

A scenario of a concrete (local) problem on access to education. There must be a flow diagram and identification of the elements at play in this scenario.

Digital Materials or Tools

Concept mapping and flowchart software: Tools such as Coogle, MindMeister or Lucidchart, which will help each teacher organise and visualise information effectively.

Internet connection: To access online resources and collaborate with your peers in real time.

Projector and screen: For theoretical presentations and the final presentation of the groups' proposals.

EDUCATIONAL SCENARIO aimed at companies

Workshop on the development of creative solutions for the use of clean energy in the business sector

Linked SDGs

Activity

Participants will develop computational and complex thinking competencies by designing innovative clean energy solutions for the business sector, aligned with SDG 7 (Affordable and Clean Energy). Through a workshop approach, employees apply concepts such as abstraction, decomposition, pattern recognition, and algorithm design to challenges like reducing carbon footprints. Using data tools and collaborative work, they analyze energy consumption, identify improvement areas, and propose feasible solutions such as solar integration or energy management systems. The activity concludes with the presentation and evaluation of proposals, fostering practical problem-solving, collaboration, and the application of computational thinking to sustainable business practices.

Objective

To train employees of companies in the business sector in the identification, development and evaluation of creative and innovative solutions for the use of clean energy using computational and complex thinking tools and techniques.

Specific Objectives

1. Promote the understanding and application of skills in abstraction, decomposition, pattern identification and algorithm design.
2. Promote collaboration between companies and students for the implementation of sustainable solutions.
3. Evaluate the impact and effectiveness of the solutions developed in the business context.

Beginning

1. Welcome and Introduction
    - Presentation of the facilitators and the objectives of the workshop.
    - Introduction to the concept of computational thinking and its importance in solving complex problems.
    - Presentation of the global problem of climate change and the need for clean energy solutions.
2. Presentation of the E4CCT Platform
    - Demonstration of the E4CCT platform functionalities, highlighting its features, including videos, quizzes and data science tools.

Development

1. Theoretical Phase
   - Abstraction and Decomposition
     - Introduction to problem decomposition techniques and their application in the business context.
     - Practical example: breaking down the problem of a high carbon footprint in a company.
2. Practical Phase
   - Identification of Patterns
     - Group exercise to identify common patterns in a company's energy consumption.
     - Use of data science tools to analyse energy consumption and detect areas for improvement.
   - Algorithm Design
     - Development of simple algorithms to optimise the use of clean energy.
     - Implementation of solutions using technologies such as solar panels and energy management systems.

Closing

1. Submission of Proposals
   - The groups will present their analyses and proposed solutions.
   - Discussion and feedback on the feasibility and applicability of solutions in the business context.
2. Evaluation and Reflection
   - Evaluation of the workshop through surveys and analytical rubrics.
   - Reflection on the lessons learned and the next steps to follow.

Evaluation

Several dimensions will be considered in the evaluation: Identifying Key Concepts, Decomposition of the problem and Feasibility of solutions in practice, using patterns and algorithms,

Evidence of Learning

1. Flowcharts and conceptual diagrams showing the breakdown of the problem and the proposed solutions.
2. Presentation of the proposals developed by the groups, demonstrating the patterns identified and the solution algorithms.

Digital Materials or Tools

1. Concept map and flowchart software: tools such as Coggle, MindMeister or Lucidchart to organise and visualise information.
2. Internet connection: to access online resources and collaborate in real time.
3. Projector and screen: for theoretical presentations and the final presentation of the proposals.

EDUCATIONAL SCENARIO aimed at NGOs

Competency development workshop on computational and complex thinking for NGOs

Linked SDGs

Activity

Participants will develop skills to design solar photovoltaic systems, bearing in mind the importance of renewable energies in the context of SDG 7 and focusing on proposals to face contemporary energy challenges. This activity ranges from the selection of components to the calculation of energy needs to learn about complex systems that handle energy, encouraging computational and complex thinking to find creative solutions and highlighting the importance of this knowledge throughout life and of the role of NGOs in its implementation.

Objective

To develop the capacity of participants to think critically and creatively about complex problems related to the management of affordable and clean energy (SDG 7), teach them to identify and apply solutions to the problem of sustainable energy supply through the design of photovoltaic systems that can be installed in their homes, and help them identify these systems' components and calculate their energy needs.

Beginning

1. Preparation and Welcome
    - The equipment is configured. it is ensured that the participants have the facilities and equipment necessary for implementation. Access to the E4C&CT platform is verified.
    - The facilitation team is introduced. This step highlights the relevance of energy sustainability for sustainable supply, not only in companies or businesses, but as part of everyday life. It also emphasises the usefulness in communities with limited resources or poor access conditions for dignified development.
2. Introduction to the Course
    - Kick-off session on the importance of renewable energy, options for promoting energy sustainability and the role of civil society and non-governmental organisations in energy lifelong education.
3. Presentation of the Case Study
    - Participants are first introduced to the components of photovoltaic systems and shown how to calculate their energy consumption through exercises.
    - Participants are presented with a case study in a rural community with modest energy consumption requirements, mainly in lighting, cooling and ventilation, but with limited access to electricity for infrastructure, meaning that they rely heavily on fossil fuels, which are expensive and harmful to the environment. Participants must decompose this problem and calculate energy consumption to propose a solution for energy use using a photocell.

Development

1. Enter the E4C&CT platform.
2. Read the case study.
3. Participants will work in groups to propose innovative solutions to problems related to sustainable energy, encouraging collaboration and the development of soft skills.
4. Analysis of the solutions found and the strategies implemented by each team and reflection on key learnings and the importance of NGOs to promote the management and use of renewable and sustainable energy resources.

Closing

Each team will comment on their experience of using computational thinking to find solutions to complex problems, reflect on their individual and group achievements during the workshop and explain what implementation options seem viable to them as NGOs.

Evaluation

Based on the case study presented on the platform, NGO participants are asked to join a team and develop a solution to the case. Key learnings acquired and their opinions on the matter are recorded on the platform through instruments that evaluate the technical content and usability of the platform.

Tests that are incorporated into the platform before and after the activity. The results will be used to measure learning, user satisfaction, and participant's solution proposals to a case study presented as a task. The instruments incorporated into the platform to gather data about the participants are the eComplexity (Castillo-Martínez & Ramírez-Montoya, 2022), and a user experience survey.

Evidence of Learning

Participants answer questionnaires that evaluate technical knowledge. A solution to the case uploaded to the platform and the forum and co-creation activities alluding to the topic of sustainable energy and design of photovoltaic systems also serve as evidence of learning.

Digital Materials or Tools

- Access to the E4C&CT platform and complementary educational resources.
- Videos, infographics and how-to guides to facilitate continuous and autonomous learning.
- Support materials and documentation to reinforce concepts learned during the course.

Reference

Castillo-Martínez, I. M. & Ramírez-Montoya, M. S. (2022). Instrumento eComplexity: Medición de la percepción de estudiantes de educación superior acerca de su competencia de razonamiento para la complejidad. https://hdl.handle.net/11285/643622

EDUCATIONAL SCENARIO aimed at lifelong learning

Competency development workshop in computational and complex thinking for lifelong learning

Linked SDGs

7 AFFORDABLE AND CLEAN ENERGY

Activity

Participants will learn the importance of renewable energies in the context of SDG 7, with a focus on proposals that tackle contemporary energy challenges based on their own life experience. This activity will develop skills related to designing solar photovoltaic systems, from the selection of components to the calculation of energy needs and encourage computational and complex thinking to face the challenges of an increasingly complex future.

Objective

To develop the capacity of participants to enable them to critically and creatively address complex problems on sustainable energy supply based on their life experience and through the design of photovoltaic systems that can be installed in homes, whose components will be identified, and energy needs will be calculated.

Beginning

Participants are motivated with a video alluding to SDG 7. They are asked to detail situations that they have experienced that are close to what they witnessed in the video. They are introduced to the facilitating team, and the relevance of energy sustainability to sustainable supply as part of daily life is highlighted.

Subsequently, they are introduced to the E4C&CT platform. They are presented with various ways of promoting energy sustainability and taught the components of photovoltaic (PV) systems and how to calculate the energy consumption of these systems through exercises. Participants will work in groups, encouraging collaboration and the development of soft skills.

Development

Participants are presented with a case study of a rural community with modest energy consumption requirements (lighting, cooling and ventilation) that has no access to electricity and is dependent on fossil fuels, which are expensive and harmful to the environment. Participants must decompose this problem and calculate energy consumption to propose a solution for energy use using a photocell.

Closing

Each team will present their solution for group discussion, comment on their experience of using computational thinking to find solutions to complex problems, reflect on their individual and group achievements during the course and contemplate the importance of managing and harnessing renewable and sustainable energy resources in preparing people for the challenges of the future.

Evaluation

Tests that are incorporated into the platform before and after the activity. The results will be used to measure learning, user satisfaction surveys, and participant's solution proposals to a case study presented as a task developed by each participant. The instruments incorporated into the platform to gather data about the participants are the: eComplexity (Castillo-Martínez & Ramírez-Montoya, 2022), and a user experience survey.

Evidence of Learning

Through forum activities, co-creation exercises and quizzes on the platform, participants can assess their technical knowledge and share their PV system design solutions.

Digital Materials or Tools

Access to the E4C&CT platform and the complementary resources it hosts, such as videos, infographics and practical guides, to facilitate continuous and autonomous learning.

Reference

Castillo-Martínez, I. M. & Ramírez-Montoya, M. S. (2022). Instrumento eComplexity: Medición de la percepción de estudiantes de educación superior acerca de su competencia de razonamiento para la complejidad. https://hdl.handle.net/11285/643622

Recommendations for Implementation

The following work plan is recommended for implementation (Figure 5).

Preparation

- Before implementation, make sure that all facilitators and participants are familiar with the platform. Conduct preliminary training sessions if necessary.

- Perform technical tests to make sure that all equipment and internet connections are working properly. Verify that all links and accesses are operational.

- Make sure each participant has their account created and set up correctly. The platform, in the registration section provides clear instructions on how to login and navigate the platform.

During Implementation

- Use all the functionalities available on the platform, such as videos, questionnaires, survey instruments and data science tools, to offer a complete and enriching experience.

- Encourage interaction and collaboration among participants through discussion forums, live chats and group work. This will help create a dynamic and participatory learning environment.

- Monitor each participant's progress regularly. Use the platform's analytics and monitoring tools to identify areas where participants may need additional support.

Post-Implementation

- Perform a thorough analysis of the data collected during deployment. Use this data to evaluate the effectiveness of the platform and the impact on each participant's computational problem-solving skills.

- Identify areas for improvement based on feedback and data analysis. Continuously update and improve the platform and training materials for future implementations.

- Share the results and learnings with all the stakeholders involved. Disseminate successes and best practices through reports, publications and presentations.

Figure 5. Recommendations for implementing the E4C&CT Digital Ecosystem platform

Real-World Application

The E4C&CT platform distinguishes itself by emphasising the application of computational and complex thinking skills to real-world challenges, offering learners practical experiences that go beyond theoretical knowledge. Through scenario-based learning, participants engage in tasks modelled after real-world situations, such as analysing energy consumption. Each scenario reflects the intricacies of global issues, often framed by the Sustainable Development Goals (SDGs).

For instance, learners may work on a project related to SDG 7, using computational thinking to develop energy-efficient solutions with renewable energy design for a community with limited access to electricity. In this scenario, participants would analyse energy consumption patterns, break down the problem into manageable components, and design algorithms to optimise energy use. These hands-on tasks simulate the decision-making processes required in professional settings, providing participants with valuable insights into how computational and complex thinking can drive innovative solutions.

By applying their skills in these real-world contexts, learners develop critical competencies in problem solving, data analysis, and systems thinking. The platform also integrates artificial intelligence tools and data analytics to provide real-time feedback, allowing learners to refine their approaches. This practical focus equips users to tackle challenges across various sectors – including education, technology, and energy – making the E4C&CT platform an invaluable resource for preparing future-ready professionals capable of addressing the world's most pressing issues.

Impact on Digital Literacy

The E4C&CT platform plays a pivotal role in enhancing digital literacy by equipping learners with the essential twenty-first-century skills needed to succeed in an increasingly technology-driven world. Through its interactive, scenario-based learning approach, the platform cultivates a deep understanding of key digital competencies such as data analysis, problem solving, and algorithmic thinking. Participants not only learn how to use digital tools but also develop the ability to critically evaluate and apply these tools to address complex, real-world problems. The integration of artificial intelligence and data science further strengthens their capacity to manage, interpret, and effectively utilise digital information. This holistic approach to digital literacy extends far beyond basic technological proficiency, empowering learners to become adaptable and innovative in response to evolving digital landscapes and professional demands. By engaging with the

E4C&CT platform, users acquire the skills necessary to navigate, contribute to, and lead within a rapidly digitising global workforce.

Inclusivity Strategies

The E4C&CT Digital Ecosystem takes significant strides in promoting inclusivity by leveraging the power of advanced accessibility tools, notably the UserWay Toolbox. UserWay is a digital accessibility solution provider that enhances the accessibility of digital platforms by incorporating AI-driven features. This toolbox plays a critical role in breaking down barriers, such as the digital divide, and ensuring that the platform reaches underserved or marginalised communities, particularly those with disabilities or limited access to technology.

The UserWay Toolbox, as shown in Figure 6, offers a wide range of functionalities to meet the need of individuals with varying accessibility requirement. These features are instrumental in fostering inclusivity by addressing different impairments, including motor, visual, cognitive, and auditory limitations. Key features of the toolbox include:

- **Motor Impaired Accessibility:** This feature improves platform usability for individuals who face challenges using a standard mouse or keyboard. Options such as larger cursors, keyboard navigation assistance, and voice command functionality ensure that individuals with motor impairments can navigate the platform seamlessly and engage with its content.
- **Screen Reader Integration:** For visually impaired users, the screen reader reads aloud the text displayed on the screen, allowing users to access content without relying on sight. This feature ensures that users who are blind or have low vision can interact with the platform without obstacles.
- **Text Customisation:** Features like larger text, contrast adjustment, and text spacing allow users with cognitive or visual impairments to tailor the text display to their needs. For users with dyslexia, the Dyslexia-Friendly Mode optimises the text display by adjusting font style and layout to enhance readability.
- **Colour Blind Assistance:** Users with colour blindness can adjust visual content using colour modification settings, making the platform accessible to individuals with various forms of colour blindness, ensuring an inclusive visual experience.
- **Seizure and Epileptic Considerations:** The Pause Animations feature ensures a safe browsing experience for individuals sensitive to flashing lights or animations by halting dynamic content that could trigger seizures.

- **ADHD and Attention Support:** Users with attention-related conditions can benefit from features such as increased text spacing and focus enhancement tools, which help maintain concentration and engagement with the platform's content.
- **Multilingual and Multimodal Access:** The platform supports multiple languages, as indicated by the language toggle in the UserWay Toolbox, enabling users from diverse linguistic backgrounds to access the platform in their preferred language. This extends the platform's reach to global communities, particularly in regions where English is not the first language.

By incorporating the UserWay Toolbox into the E4C&CT platform, we address not only physical and cognitive barriers but also those created by the digital divide. These features ensure that users from marginalised communities – whether they have disabilities or live in regions with limited access to educational resources – can fully engage with the platform and benefit from its educational content. This integration supports the overarching goal of inclusivity, aligning with the Sustainable Development Goals (SDGs) by promoting equitable access to quality education.

In summary, the UserWay Toolbox ensures that the E4C&CT platform is accessible to a diverse range of users, allowing the ecosystem to provide meaningful educational experiences to all, regardless of their physical, cognitive, or linguistic limitations. These inclusivity strategies position the platform to break down barriers and offer an accessible and equitable learning environment for all users.

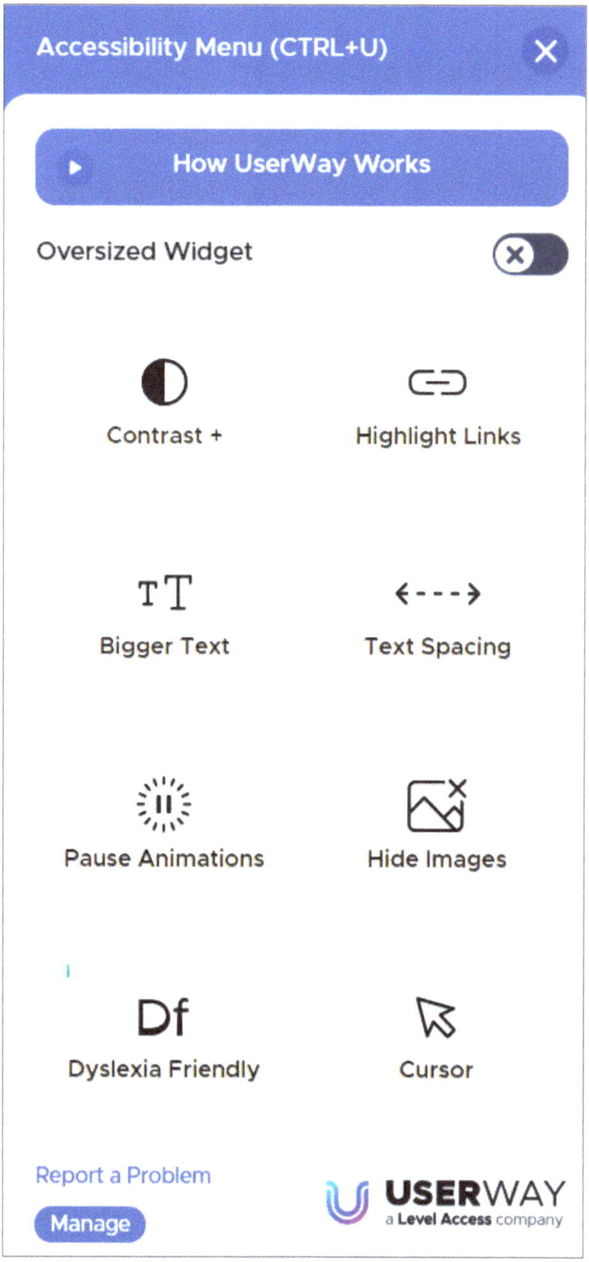

Figure 6. UserWay integration within E4C&CT

OPEN EDUCATIONAL RESOURCES (OER)

OER: The E4CCT Ecosystem: An Open Educational Ecosystem for Collaboration and Training.
Author: Irma Azeneth Patiño Zúñiga.
Reference: Patiño Zúñiga, I. A. (2024). *The E4CCT Ecosystem: An open educational ecosystem for collaboration and training* [Video]. https://hdl.handle.net/11285/676170

▶ We share with you an educational video resource that will take you on a fascinating journey through a digital ecosystem designed to develop computational thinking and complex reasoning skills. This video provides an overview of the E4CCT project, including its objectives, methodology and the transformative impact it has had on education. Throughout the video, we will learn how these personalised learning tools, tailored to each student's individual abilities, promote critical and complex thinking skills, significantly improving educational quality. Join this experience and let's discover how we can boost learning and prepare students for the challenges of the future together. Let's co-build!

OER: STEM Roadmap for Mobilising Open Education.
Authors: María Soledad Ramírez-Montoya, Carolina Alcantar Nieblas & José Vladimir Burgos Aguilar.
Reference: Ramírez-Montoya, M. S., Alcantar Nieblas, C., & Burgos Aguilar, J. V. (2024). *STEM Roadmap for Mobilising Open Education* [Video]. https://hdl.handle.net/11285/676163

▶ We invite you to join us in a unique experience through this educational video resource that presents the fascinating STEM Roadmap to Mobilise Open Education and guides us through the exciting application process to the STEM Roadmap 2024 programme. This video details the programme, its objectives and the necessary steps to participate. Through this resource, we will understand how this initiative can transform our educational opportunities and open new doors in the world of science, technology, engineering and mathematics. Join us on this learning adventure, and let's discover how we can be part of this innovative programme together. Let's build in a network!

OER: Programming the Future: Digital Escape Rooms.
Authors: José Martín Molina Espinosa & Paloma Suárez Brito.
Reference: Molina Espinosa, J. M. & Suárez-Brito, P. (2023). Programming the Future: Digital Escape Rooms [Video]. *Webcast program: Future of education in complexity.* Tecnológico de Monterrey. https://repositorio.tec.mx/handle/11285/651632

▶ We share with you this educational video resource on the exciting experience of using digital escape in higher education to assess computational and complex thinking skills. Imagine that we are sitting together, listening to Paloma Suárez and Martín Molina in an inspiring panel, who tell us how these dynamics of digital escape can transform our teaching methodologies. Through this resource, we'll discover how these interactive tools not only make learning more fun but also allow us to effectively measure crucial skills in our students. Join this learning community, and let's discover new ways of teaching and assessing together. Let's learn together!

OER: Breaking Codes and Building Computational Thinking Skills.
Authors: Román Martínez & Amadeo Argüelles.
Reference: Martínez, R. & Argüelles, A. (2023). Breaking codes and building computational thinking skills [Video]. *Webcast program: Future of education in complexity.* Tecnológico de Monterrey. https://hdl.handle.net/11285/676176

▶ We invite you on a fascinating journey through a video educational resource that you can't miss. This video, titled 'Breaking Codes and Building Computational Thinking Skills', introduces us to an innovative technology platform designed for higher education students. In this video, Román Mendoza and Amadeo Argüelles explain in detail what this tool is, how it works and what it is used for. Through the video, we will understand the importance of computational thinking in the business environment and how this platform can equip students with essential skills for the future. Join us on this exciting exploration, and let's find out how we can leverage this technology to enhance our education and career readiness together. Let's grow in community!

OER: Detecting Generative Artificial Intelligence Essays using Large Language Models: Machine and Deep Learning Approaches.
Authors: Rasikh Tariq, Fidel Antonio Guadalupe Casillas-Muñoz, Muhammad Ashraf Waqar & María Soledad Ramírez-Montoya.
Reference: Tariq, R., Casillas-Muñoz, F., Ashraf, W. M., & Ramírez-Montoya, M. S. (2024). Detecting Generative Artificial Intelligence Essays using Large Language Models: Machine and Deep Learning Approaches [Text]. In *2024 International Conference on Engineering & Computing Technologies* (ICECT) (pp. 1–6). IEEE. Handle: https://hdl.handle.net/11285/675892

▶ We want to invite you to explore this educational text resource that addresses a fascinating and very relevant topic: how to detect essays generated by artificial intelligence using advanced machine and deep learning models. This study focuses on distinguishing between human-written and AI-generated essays and highlights the ethical implications in academia. Here, we will discuss how algorithms, such as logistic regression, support vector machine (SVM), decision trees, random forests, K-Nearest Neighbours (KNN) and Long Short-Term Memory (LSTM) are used to develop models that classify trials. You'll learn about the Term Frequency-Inverse Document Frequency (TF-IDF) technique, which assesses the importance of words in a document, and how parameters are fine-tuned to ensure model accuracy. The findings highlight SVM's accuracy and ability to accurately classify assays, while decision trees, while straightforward, present a higher risk of misclassification. KNN and random forests offer a good balance, and LSTM excels at contextual understanding, although it requires more computational resources. This study underscores the importance of selecting the right algorithm to maintain academic integrity and fostering genuine student creativity. Join us on this learning adventure, and let's discover new learning together!

Conclusion

In an era where global challenges are increasingly complex and interconnected, developing computational and complex thinking skills is essential. The E4C&CT Digital Ecosystem platform emerges as a transformative educational tool designed to bridge the gap between theoretical knowledge and practical application. By integrating scenario-based learning aligned with the Sustainable Development Goals (SDGs), the platform equips learners with the competencies necessary to navigate and address real-world problems effectively.

Throughout this guide, we have explored how the E4C&CT platform fosters an interdisciplinary approach, linking computational thinking with complex reasoning to provide a holistic learning experience. The platform's unique incorporation of advanced technologies such as artificial intelligence and data science not only enhances digital literacy but also personalises the learning journey for each participant. This ensures that learners from diverse backgrounds can access, engage with, and benefit from the platform, thus promoting inclusivity and equity in education.

The E4C&CT platform represents a significant advancement in educational innovation by bridging the gap between theoretical knowledge and the practical application of computational and complex thinking skills. By immersing learners in real-world scenarios aligned with the Sustainable Development Goals, it prepares them to tackle the complexities of modern global challenges effectively. The platform's unique integration of advanced technologies, such as artificial intelligence and data science, further strengthens digital literacy, fostering essential twenty-first-century competencies.

Anticipated long-term impacts include transforming educational practices, influencing policy development, and empowering a diverse generation of problem-solvers equipped to drive sustainable development worldwide. By offering an inclusive and accessible learning ecosystem, the E4C&CT platform has the potential to make a lasting, positive impact on both individuals and society, shaping a future where innovative thinking leads to meaningful change.

CALL TO ACTION

Would you like to participate in the project?
Welcome to the exciting project of designing and evaluating a state-of-the-art digital ecosystem!

Let us present you with a unique opportunity to improve your problem-solving skills by fostering computational thinking. Please contact us through the E4CTT platform (https://e4cct.mx) for suggestions and collaboration options for generating a cutting-edge tool that includes artificial intelligence, machine learning and data science.

Imagine having access to a digital ecosystem where you can diagnose, develop and assess your complex thinking skills to face both your studies and the challenges of life, all in one place. Whether you're a college student, a professional looking to improve your complex thinking skills or just someone with an interest in boosting your skills in this field, we've got something amazing for you! Don't miss the opportunity to be part of this exciting project. Join us and be part of the education revolution through this digital ecosystem.

We will collaboratively take your skills to new heights!
Our research group: https://tec.mx/es/r4c-irg
Explore our projects: https://www.research4challenges.world/

Join the E4C&CT Digital Ecosystem project:
https://www.research4challenges.world/computationalthink

GLOSSARY

Decomposition: A pillar of computational thinking that involves breaking down complex problems into smaller, more manageable components.

Computational Thinking: A problem-solving process that involves breaking down a large problem into smaller, more manageable parts, identifying patterns, abstracting irrelevant details and designing algorithms (a series of steps) to find efficient solutions. It is a fundamental skill in computer science and can be applied in many areas beyond programming. For example, imagine organising a party. First, you break the task down into smaller parts: choosing a date, making a guest list, planning the menu and arranging decorations. Next, you identify patterns from previous parties that were successful, such as preferred food and music choices. Irrelevant details, like considering only guests who live nearby, would then be abstracted. Finally, you create a step-by-step plan to carry out each task, making sure everything is ready on time. This mirrors how a programmer would approach a complex problem using computational thinking.

Complex Thinking: The ability to comprehend and manage problems or situations that encompass multiple interrelated components and lack a singular, simple solution. It requires considering different perspectives, recognising connections between different elements and anticipating the consequences of different actions. For instance, managing a project to reduce pollution in a city involves not only identifying pollution sources (such as factories and traffic) but also understanding how proposed measures (such as regulating industrial emissions or promoting bicycle use) will impact the economy, public health and daily life. Complex thinking entails balancing the needs of different stakeholders (citizens, businesses, government) and formulating solutions that minimise pollution without causing other serious problems. This ability to navigate and resolve multifaceted situations is the essence of complex thinking.

Open Educational Resource: Teaching, learning or research materials that are in the public domain or published under intellectual property licences that facilitate their use, adaptation and distribution free of charge.

5.0 Technologies: Emerging technologies associated with the fifth industrial revolution, emphasising collaboration between humans and machines, including advanced AI, robotics, and data analytics.

Abstraction: The process of reducing complexity by focusing on the main idea and ignoring specific details, making problems easier to understand and solve.

Algorithm: A step-by-step set of instructions designed to perform a specific task or solve a problem efficiently.

Algorithmic Thinking: The ability to create a series of ordered steps to solve a problem or perform a task, fundamental to computational thinking.

Artificial Intelligence (AI): The simulation of human intelligence processes by machines, enabling them to perform tasks that typically require human intelligence, such as learning and problem solving.

Data Analytics: The science of analysing raw data to draw meaningful insights and inform decision-making.

Data Mining: The process of discovering patterns and relationships in large datasets to extract valuable information.

Data Science: An interdisciplinary field that combines statistics, computer science, and domain expertise to extract knowledge and insights from data.

Decision Trees: A flowchart-like model used in decision-making and machine learning that maps out possible outcomes of a series of related choices.

Decomposition: A fundamental computational thinking skill involving breaking down complex problems into smaller, more manageable parts.

Deep Learning: A subset of machine learning involving neural networks with many layers that can learn complex patterns in large amounts of data.

Digital Literacy: The ability to effectively use digital tools and technologies to find, evaluate, create, and communicate information.

Educational Data Mining: The practice of analysing data from educational settings to improve learning outcomes and understand student behaviour.

Educational Interventions: Strategies or programmes implemented to improve educational outcomes or address specific learning challenges.

Equitable Education: Education that is fair and inclusive, providing equal learning opportunities regardless of students' backgrounds or abilities.

Gamification: The application of game-design elements in non-game contexts to engage and motivate people to achieve their goals.

Inclusive Education: An educational approach where all students, regardless of their abilities or disabilities, learn together in the same age-appropriate classroom.

K-Nearest Neighbours (KNN): A simple machine learning algorithm used for classification and regression by analysing the 'k' closest data points.

Learning Analytics: The collection and analysis of data about learners to improve education quality and personalise learning experiences.

Logistic Regression: A statistical method for analysing datasets in which there are one or more independent variables that determine an outcome, used for binary classification tasks.

Long Short-Term Memory (LSTM): A type of neural network architecture capable of learning order dependence in sequence prediction problems.

Machine Learning: A subset of AI that enables computers to learn from data and improve their performance over time without being explicitly programmed.

Micro-Certificate: A credential representing the completion of a short course or specific skill set, often stackable towards a larger qualification.

Pattern Recognition: Identifying and analysing patterns or regularities in data, essential for predicting future data trends.

Phylogenetics: The study of evolutionary relationships among biological entities, often represented through a 'family tree' of species.

Random Forests: A machine learning technique that builds multiple decision trees and merges them to get a more accurate and stable prediction.

Scenario-Based Learning: An instructional design approach that uses interactive scenarios to support active learning and apply knowledge in real-world contexts.

Support Vector Machine (SVM): A supervised machine learning algorithm used for classification and regression tasks by finding the best boundary that separates classes.

Sustainable Development Goals (SDGs): A collection of seventeen global goals set by the United Nations to address pressing challenges like poverty, inequality, and climate change by 2030.

Term Frequency-Inverse Document Frequency (TF-IDF): A numerical statistic used to reflect how important a word is to a document in a collection, commonly used in text mining.

Text Mining: The process of deriving meaningful information from natural language text, often involving computational analysis to identify patterns.

Transition Design Approach: A framework for addressing complex societal problems by envisioning and facilitating systemic change over time.

Virtual Reality (VR): A computer-generated simulation of a three-dimensional environment that can be interacted with using special electronic equipment.

WebVR: An open standard that enables virtual reality experiences within a web browser, making VR accessible without specialised applications.

Twenty-First-Century Competencies: Essential skills for success in today's world, including critical thinking, creativity, collaboration, communication, and digital literacy.

Contenidos

Impulsa tu Pensamiento Computacional y Razonamiento Complejo

Plataforma de ecosistema digital E4C&CT

Figura 1.
Investigadores del R4C-IRG movilizadores de la plataforma ecosistema digital E4C&CT

Sobre Nosotros

Somos integrantes del grupo de investigación R4C-IRG Escalando el pensamiento complejo para todos (Figura 1), nos apasiona llevar la educación superior a nuevos niveles de excelencia. Nos dedicamos a desarrollar y promover competencias avanzadas de razonamiento para enfrentar la complejidad del mundo moderno. Utilizamos estrategias de Ciencia Abierta y las más avanzadas Tecnologías 5.0, como la inteligencia artificial y la ciencia de datos, para crear sistemas formativos que preparen a las personas para los desafíos del futuro. Nuestra labor se enlaza con proyectos que integran la universidad, la industria, el gobierno y el sector civil, buscando siempre soluciones sostenibles que beneficien a toda la sociedad.

Nuestra visión es clara y ambiciosa: contribuir de manera significativa al futuro de la educación, creando soluciones innovadoras para los problemas y retos de la sociedad actual. Nos alineamos con los objetivos de la agenda 2030 de la Unesco para el desarrollo sostenible, fomentando la colaboración interdisciplinaria y la construcción de redes académicas robustas. En R4C-IRG, trabajamos para formar una nueva generación de profesionales altamente competitivos y comprometidos con el bienestar social, siempre buscando habilitar soluciones innovadoras que respondan a los retos presentes y futuros.

Carta editorial

Visualicemos una nueva forma de pensar que conecta a seres humanos con máquinas: el pensamiento computacional. Este enfoque revolucionario nos permite descomponer problemas complejos en partes manejables, encontrar patrones y crear soluciones eficientes utilizando la lógica y el razonamiento sistemático. Al adoptar el pensamiento computacional, no solo mejoraremos nuestras habilidades para interactuar con la tecnología, sino que también desarrollaremos una mentalidad que nos capacita para enfrentar los desafíos del siglo XXI de manera innovadora y eficaz.

Nuestro proyecto desarrolla un ecosistema digital, una plataforma llamada E4C&CT: para escalar el pensamiento computacional, desde la que se presentan escenarios del mundo real con diferentes niveles de complejidad. Con herramientas de inteligencia artificial gestionamos y visualizamos los datos, aplicamos procesos de análisis inteligentes para estudiar cómo las personas usuarias de ciencias computacionales resuelven problemas. Es como si estuviéramos creando un laboratorio virtual donde podemos observar, aprender y mejorar nuestras habilidades juntos.

El pensamiento computacional no es solo una habilidad técnica; es una nueva forma de alfabetización que todas las personas debemos adquirir. En un mundo cada vez más sustentado en la tecnología, comprender cómo funcionan los algoritmos y cómo podemos utilizarlos para resolver problemas nos da una ventaja competitiva y nos prepara para un futuro incierto pero lleno de posibilidades. Pero los beneficios no terminan ahí. Las instituciones educativas y las personas responsables de la toma de decisiones también se ven beneficiadas, ya que los resultados de nuestra investigación pueden guiar futuras intervenciones educativas y responder al creciente mercado de la educación y el análisis del aprendizaje. Además, planeamos colaborar con los principales centros de investigación del mundo, lo que significa que estaremos creando una comunidad global dedicada a mejorar la educación y la tecnología.

¡Te invitamos a ser parte de esta emocionante aventura y a construir juntos un futuro lleno de innovación y colaboración!

OBJETIVOS

Nuestro objetivo principal es diseñar y evaluar un ecosistema digital que emule entornos del mundo real. Este ecosistema utiliza herramientas como la inteligencia artificial, el aprendizaje automático y la ciencia de datos para diagnosticar, desarrollar y evaluar las habilidades de resolución de problemas computacionales en estudiantes universitarios. Queremos ayudarte a mejorar tu capacidad de pensar de manera compleja y computacional, no sólo para estudiar, sino para los retos que se presentan a lo largo de la vida.

Objetivos específicos

1 Desarrollar una plataforma que integra procedimientos de enseñanza para comprender la resolución de problemas computacionales con herramientas automatizadas basadas en análisis de aprendizaje, inteligencia artificial, juegos, aprendizaje automático y ciencia de datos. Estas herramientas nos permiten analizar comportamientos y mejorar nuestras habilidades de razonamiento complejo.

2 Implementar y evaluar el ecosistema digital en instituciones de educación superior de América Latina y de habla hispana, diagnosticando, desarrollando y evaluando las habilidades de estudiantes en resolución de problemas y razonamiento complejo a través de métodos cuantitativos y cualitativos. Además, validamos el desempeño del ecosistema en términos de capacidades tecnológicas y experiencia del usuario.

3 Registrar licenciamientos de derechos de autor, metodologías, contenidos y conocimientos para transferir la propiedad intelectual a través de una startup.

Figura 2.
Objetivos generales y específicos del proyecto E4C&CT: ecosistema para ampliar los pensamientos computacional y complejo

Objetivos

Introducción

¿Sabías que el 65 % de las personas que en la actualidad estudian, en el futuro trabajarán en empleos que aún no existen? (Computerworld University, 2016). En un mundo donde la tecnología avanza a pasos agigantados, la forma en que enseñamos habilidades de pensamiento computacional es más crucial que nunca. El pensamiento computacional es una habilidad fundamental que consiste en abstraer problemas y formular soluciones que puedan automatizarse. Cada vez se reconoce más que es esencial en una sociedad basada en la información, la enseñanza de la ciencia, la tecnología, la ingeniería y las matemáticas. No se trata solo de saber programar computadoras, sino de aplicar métodos y técnicas de la informática para encontrar soluciones eficientes y lógicas. Por ejemplo, implica descomponer un problema grande en partes más pequeñas y manejables, encontrar patrones y seguir procesos paso a paso.

El pensamiento computacional es una habilidad esencial en la era digital, pero muchos programas educativos aún no lo abordan de manera efectiva. Este ecosistema que integra recursos educativos abiertos tiene como objetivo llenar ese vacío. Para lograrlo, se ha diseñado y desarrollado la plataforma E4C&CT que simula situaciones reales de distintas complejidades para enseñar pensamiento computacional de manera práctica y efectiva a un amplio espectro de profesionales y público en general. El objetivo es mejorar en las personas las habilidades de resolución de problemas, al hacerlo, nos preparamos para enfrentar los retos del siglo XXI en diferentes áreas. Estudios previos (Melro et al., 2023, Su y Yang, 2023) han intentado abordar estos problemas con métodos más teóricos, pero nuestro enfoque práctico y contextualizado promete ser más efectivo y prepararnos para actuar en diferentes escenarios presentes y futuros (Figura 3). Además, las personas responsables de la toma de decisiones en el sector educativo podrán utilizar los resultados de esta investigación para diseñar intervenciones educativas más efectivas y adaptadas a las necesidades actuales. Esto es especialmente importante para estudiantes con necesidades especiales o aquellos que habiten en contextos desfavorecidos, garantizando así una educación más inclusiva y equitativa.

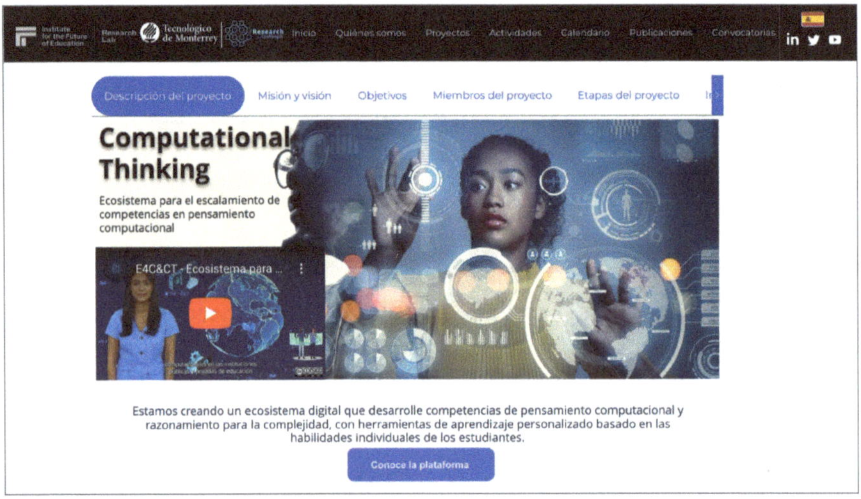

Figura 3. Página web del proyecto E4C&CT
https://www.research4challenges.world/computationalthink

La plataforma E4C&CT incorpora escenarios relacionados con varios Objetivos de Desarrollo Sostenible, dirigidos específicamente a problemas globales como la salud, el agua, la energía, la educación y las desigualdades. Esta plataforma utiliza un enfoque de pensamiento computacional y mejora el pensamiento complejo a través del aprendizaje basado en escenarios. Evolucionando continuamente mediante la inteligencia artificial y la minería de datos educativos, ofrece una experiencia única para participantes de diversos orígenes, particularmente en países de habla hispana. La plataforma cuenta con un diseño instruccional distintivo inspirado en la gamificación que incluye foros interactivos, aprendizaje basado en proyectos y estudios de caso, Recursos Educativos Abiertos (REA), junto con videos educativos e instructivos. Este diseño promueve un entorno de aprendizaje atractivo donde los estudiantes pueden practicar habilidades como la abstracción, identificación de patrones, descomposición y pensamiento algorítmico.

Como una plataforma de acceso abierto sin restricciones geográficas, ofrece un recorrido completo desde la evaluación previa hasta la evaluación posterior, conduciendo a múltiples experiencias de aprendizaje basadas en proyectos y culminando en un microcertificado, todo gestionado dentro de la plataforma. Este material tiene el potencial de redefinir el futuro de la educación al integrar el pensamiento computacional en el aprendizaje. Al seguir innovando, podemos asegurarnos de que las futuras generaciones desarrollen las competencias para hacer frente a los desafíos y oportunidades del mundo digital. Innovar en educación no es solo una opción, sino una necesidad para construir una sociedad más inclusiva y preparada para el futuro.

A pesar del creciente énfasis en el desarrollo de habilidades de pensamiento computacional en diversos contextos educativos, muchos de los enfoques actuales siguen siendo muy teóricos y carecen de un marco práctico y contextualizado que prepare a los alumnos para enfrentarse a las complejidades del mundo real. Las plataformas y programas existentes no suelen integrar escenarios del mundo real que fomenten el pensamiento computacional y complejo, habilidades esenciales para abordar los retos globales contemporáneos. Este proyecto pretende cubrir este vacío presentando el ecosistema digital E4C&CT, que combina el aprendizaje basado en escenarios con tecnologías de vanguardia como la inteligencia artificial y la ciencia de datos, para aumentar las habilidades de pensamiento computacional en diversas disciplinas.

Lo que distingue a la plataforma E4C&CT es su aplicación de escenarios reales simulados que se alinean con los objetivos de desarrollo sostenible (ODS) de las Naciones Unidas, animando a los estudiantes a comprometerse con los desafíos globales en materia de salud, energía, educación y equidad. A diferencia de los programas convencionales de pensamiento computacional que se centran únicamente en técnicas abstractas de resolución de problemas, nuestra plataforma promueve un enfoque interdisciplinar. Este método vincula el pensamiento computacional con el pensamiento complejo, dotando a los alumnos de la capacidad de abordar problemas polifacéticos mediante una combinación de análisis crítico, pensamiento sistémico y estrategias algorítmicas. La plataforma E4C&CT va más allá de la codificación y el cálculo computacional, ofreciendo una experiencia de aprendizaje práctica y completa diseñada para preparar a las personas para carreras emergentes en un panorama digital en rápida evolución.

Además, la plataforma enfatiza la accesibilidad y la inclusión. Mientras que muchos recursos educativos están limitados geográfica o económicamente, E4C&CT está diseñada para ser abierta, accesible y adaptable a diversos grupos de alumnos, incluidos los procedentes de entornos desfavorecidos. Al incorporar herramientas inspiradas en la gamificación y la inteligencia artificial, la plataforma proporciona experiencias de aprendizaje personalizadas, en las que los participantes pueden seguir su progreso a medida que navegan por diversas etapas de complejidad. Esto la convierte en un recurso muy eficaz para educadores y responsables de la toma de decisiones, ya que ofrece información valiosa que puede servir de base para futuras intervenciones y políticas educativas.

En resumen, este proyecto cubre una laguna crítica al ofrecer una solución innovadora, práctica y escalable para fomentar las capacidades de pensamiento computacional y pensamiento complejo. No solo prepara a las personas para los futuros mercados laborales, sino que también contribuye a los objetivos más amplios de una educación equitativa y de calidad, tal y como establecen los ODS. Al ofrecer un enfoque único de la educación, la plataforma E4C&CT está preparada para transformar la forma en que enseñamos y aprendemos en la era digital, garantizando que las generaciones futuras estén preparadas para hacer afrontar los retos más apremiantes del mundo.

Referencias

Computerworld University (2016). *El 65% de los trabajos de 2023 todavía no existen.* https://www.computerworlduniversity.es/actualidad/el-65-de-los-trabajos-de-2023-todavia-no-existen

Melro, A., Tarling, G., Fujita, T. y Kleine Staarman, J. (2023). What Else Can Be Learned When Coding? A Configurative Literature Review of Learning Opportunities Through Computational Thinking. *Journal of Educational Computing Research, 61*(4), 901–924. https://doi.org/10.1177/07356331221133822

Su, J. y Yang, W. (2023). A systematic review of integrating computational thinking in early childhood education. *Computers and Education Open, 4*, 100122. https://doi.org/10.1016/j.caeo.2023.100122

¿Cómo se Vincula el Pensamiento Complejo Con el Pensamiento Computacional?

El pensamiento complejo es una manera de entender la realidad, viendo las situaciones como un todo interconectado y reconociendo la influencia mutua de múltiples factores. No se trata de dividir los problemas en partes aisladas, sino de considerar cómo todos los elementos interactúan y se afectan entre sí. Por otro lado, el pensamiento computacional se centra en descomponer problemas en pasos más pequeños y manejables, utilizando la lógica y los algoritmos para encontrar soluciones eficientes.

Combinar el pensamiento complejo con el pensamiento computacional puede ayudarnos a abordar desafíos complejos como los planteados en los Objetivos de Desarrollo Sostenible, por ejemplo, la salud, la educación, las desigualdades. Al unir el pensamiento complejo con el pensamiento computacional, podemos tener una visión más completa y detallada de los problemas y la búsqueda de alternativas.

El potencial del pensamiento complejo es que nos permite ver los problemas desde múltiples ángulos, considerando todas sus variables y relaciones. A su vez, el pensamiento computacional nos brinda las herramientas para descomponer esos problemas en pasos más pequeños y manejables, utilizando la lógica y los algoritmos para encontrar soluciones eficientes. Al unir estas dos habilidades, podemos abordar los desafíos más complicados de manera más efectiva, creativa y estructurada.

El pensamiento computacional complementa y enriquece al pensamiento complejo al ofrecer herramientas para desglosar problemas complejos en componentes más manejables y solucionables, un proceso conocido como descomposición. Esencialmente, fomenta la formulación de soluciones paso a paso (algoritmos), lo que facilita la identificación de patrones y la abstracción de conceptos más allá de los datos concretos. Esta capacidad de análisis y síntesis es crucial cuando se enfrentan problemas complejos en áreas como la tecnología, la ciencia y la matemática, permitiendo a cada persona aplicar una lógica estructurada y sistemática. Al integrar el pensamiento computacional con el pensamiento complejo, se potencia la habilidad para anticipar consecuencias, evaluar múltiples soluciones posibles y aplicar enfoques innovadores y eficientes en la resolución de problemas del mundo real.

PARA SABER MÁS...
sobre pensamiento complejo y pensamiento computacional

La mente bien ordenada: repensar la reforma, reformar el pensamiento

Autor: Edgar Morin.

Referencia: Morin, E. (2020). *La mente bien ordenada: repensar la reforma, reformar el pensamiento.* Siglo XXI.

▶ Este libro propone principios esenciales para entender cómo cada parte de un problema se conecta con el todo, y viceversa. Morin nos guía a través de una visión que supera el conocimiento fragmentado, revelando las interacciones invisibles entre las partes y el todo, y abordando los problemas esenciales desde una perspectiva integral. Este enfoque no solo enriquece nuestra comprensión científica, sino que también une el pensamiento científico con el humanista, creando una visión más completa y reflexiva de nuestro destino humano. Al reformar nuestra manera de pensar, podemos organizar el conocimiento de manera que unamos estas dos culturas, tradicionalmente separadas. Así, la enseñanza se transforma en un proceso que no solo llena nuestras mentes, sino que las ordena, enseñándonos sobre la condición humana, a vivir plenamente, a enfrentar la incertidumbre y a ser ciudadanos responsables. Te invitamos a leer este libro y descubrir cómo el pensamiento complejo y el pensamiento computacional pueden integrarse para mejorar tanto nuestra educación como nuestra comprensión del mundo.

Aprendizaje de los componentes del pensamiento computacional mediado por una aplicación virtual de la educación 4.0 en el entorno del pensamiento complejo

Autores: Carlos Enrique George-Reyes, Jessica Alejandra Ruiz-Ramírez, Yessica Betzabe Contreras Fuentes y Edgar Omar López-Caudana.

Referencia: George-Reyes, C., Contreras, Y., Ruiz-Ramírez, J. y López-Caudana, E. (2023). Aprendizaje de los componentes del pensamiento computacional mediado por una aplicación virtual de la educación 4.0 en el entorno del pensamiento complejo. *Educar* 59(2), 1–20. https://doi.org/10.5565/rev/educar.1645 https://hdl.handle.net/11285/650977

▶ Este fascinante estudio presenta cómo la Educación 4.0 y sus aplicaciones, como la realidad virtual basada en la web (WebVR), pueden revolucionar el aprendizaje. Se evaluó la aceptación y el rendimiento académico de 258 estudiantes que participaron en un *rally* de conocimientos diseñado en un mundo virtual tridimensional. A través de esta investigación, se demostró que los escenarios de realidad simulada no solo fomentan la interacción y el desarrollo de competencias comunicativas y de colaboración, sino que también mejoran el rendimiento académico. Los resultados mostraron una alta aceptación de estos entornos virtuales como espacios de aprendizaje. Sin embargo, también se identificaron desafíos, como la necesidad de computadoras con alta capacidad de procesamiento y el desarrollo de habilidades digitales tanto para docentes como para estudiantes.

Modelo abierto de pensamiento complejo para el futuro de la educación

Autores: María Soledad Ramírez- Montoya, Fabián Eduardo Basabe, Martina Carlos Arroyo, Irma Azeneth Patiño Zúñiga, I. A. y May Portuguez Castro.

Referencia: Ramírez-Montoya, M. S., Basabe, E., Carlos Arroyo, M., Patiño Zúñiga, I. A., Portuguez Castro, M. (2024). *Modelo abierto de pensamiento complejo para el futuro de la educación*. Octaedro. https://hdl.handle.net/11285/652033

▶ Para descubrir más sobre pensamiento complejo, te invitamos a explorar un enfoque educativo innovador que se presenta en este texto. Este enfoque está diseñado para responder a las demandas del mundo moderno, integrando diversas dimensiones del pensamiento —crítico, científico, sistémico e innovador—. El objetivo es formar ciudadanos empáticos y comprometidos con el desarrollo sostenible. Este modelo no solo se aplica en ambientes académicos, sino también en sectores gubernamentales y empresariales, destacando la importancia de la colaboración, la empatía y el compromiso con soluciones sostenibles a problemas globales. Al sumergirte en este enfoque, podrás desarrollar habilidades que te permitirán contribuir de manera significativa a la sociedad y al bienestar del planeta.

Innovación Educativa en Acción

Plataforma E4C&CT

La educación está en constante evolución, adaptándose a las necesidades cambiantes de la sociedad y del mercado laboral. En este contexto, la plataforma E4C&CT (https://e4cct.mx/) surge como una herramienta innovadora que busca desarrollar las habilidades de pensamiento computacional a través del reconocimiento de los retos vinculados a los Objetivos de Desarrollo Sostenible (ODS). Esta plataforma educativa ofrece cursos diseñados específicamente para fomentar estas habilidades esenciales para el siglo XXI. Escanea el siguiente código QR para acceder a la plataforma:

E4C&CT: un Ecosistema de Aprendizaje

E4C&CT integra una serie de cursos enfocados en distintos retos relacionados a los ODS. Los cursos incluyen, entre otros:

- Trazando Salud. Epidemiología y filogenética.
  Este curso se enfoca en el entendimiento de la salud pública y la genética de las enfermedades, promoviendo la investigación y el análisis de datos epidemiológicos.

- EduInnovaTech. Descomponiendo retos para una educación de calidad. Diseñado para abordar los desafíos en el ámbito educativo, este curso busca mejorar la calidad de la educación a través de la innovación y la tecnología.
- SolarCT. Pensamiento computacional y energía. Curso enfocado en el uso del pensamiento computacional para resolver problemas relacionados con la energía sostenible, este curso fomenta la creación de soluciones innovadoras para la gestión y aprovechamiento de recursos energéticos.
- Equality4all. Reducción de desigualdades aplicando pensamiento complejo. Este curso aborda las desigualdades sociales y económicas, enseñando a estudiantes cómo aplicar el pensamiento complejo para desarrollar estrategias inclusivas y equitativas.

Enfoque práctico y experiencia real en los cursos de E4C&CT

Los cursos ofrecidos en E4C&CT van más allá de la teoría, promoviendo la práctica y la aplicación de conocimientos en proyectos reales. Cada estudiante puede trabajar en equipo, desarrollar prototipos y presentar sus ideas ante un panel de personas expertas. Este enfoque práctico les brinda experiencia concreta y los prepara para enfrentar los desafíos del mundo actual.

Escalamiento del pensamiento complejo

El pensamiento complejo es una habilidad esencial para aprender sobre los Objetivos de Desarrollo Sostenible (ODS). Esta habilidad permite a las personas analizar situaciones complicadas, identificar problemas y encontrar soluciones innovadoras. En E4C&CT, nos enfocamos en desarrollar este tipo de pensamiento a través de actividades y ejercicios desafiantes. Utilizamos estudios de caso, simulaciones y proyectos interdisciplinarios para enseñar a cada estudiante a abordar problemas desde diferentes ángulos, ayudándolos a encontrar soluciones integrales y efectivas.

Desarrollando el pensamiento complejo para los ODS

Los cursos de E4C&CT están diseñados para inspirar a estudiantes a crear iniciativas que generen un impacto positivo en sus comunidades y el mundo. Estos cursos abordan temas cruciales como la salud pública, la educación de calidad, la energía sostenible y la reducción de desigualdades, proporcionando a cada estudiante las herramientas necesarias para diseñar y ejecutar proyectos que aborden problemas globales críticos. Al finalizar estos cursos, cada estudiante no solo ha desarrollado habilidades de pensamiento computacional, sino que también ha adquirido una comprensión profunda de cómo sus acciones pueden contribuir al logro de los ODS impactando de manera positiva en la sociedad.

Implementación exitosa en universidades

Como parte de sus múltiples implementaciones, E4C&CT invitó a estudiantes de humanidades, ingeniería, salud, administración y economía, así como en escuelas de formación de profesores de enseñanza media (EFPEM) de Guatemala, Perú, Panamá, Colombia, Chile y Costa Rica a participar en una experiencia formativa extracurricular llamada "SolarCT: Pensamiento Computacional y Energía". Durante 2024, 927 estudiantes de las universidades participaron en esta experiencia, con resultados muy positivos: se observó un aumento significativo en sus habilidades de pensamiento computacional y en su capacidad para aplicar el pensamiento complejo en proyectos reales.

E4C&CT representa un avance importante en la educación para los Objetivos de Desarrollo Sostenible (ODS), ofreciendo un entorno de aprendizaje dinámico y práctico que prepara a cada estudiante para los desafíos del mundo real. Al combinar cursos de salud, educación, energía y equidad con un enfoque en el desarrollo de habilidades de pensamiento computacional y complejo, esta plataforma se posiciona como una herramienta indispensable para formar a la próxima generación de personas líderes. La implementación en la Universidad San Carlos de Guatemala destaca su efectividad y potencial para transformar el ecosistema educativo y contribuir al logro de los ODS en diversos contextos.

¿QUÉ DICEN LOS ESTUDIOS?

sobre la propuesta que se realiza desde el proyecto de innovación

Sabemos que vivimos en un mundo digitalizado, y por tanto el pensamiento computacional es cada vez más necesario y relevante, no basta con utilizar la computadora, cada vez es más común desarrollar actividades en línea para aprender y para saber. Una plataforma educativa diseñada específicamente para ayudarnos puede guiarnos en el entendimiento y comprensión de problemas complejos, volverlos más manejables y poder generar patrones de entendimiento o algoritmos para resolverlos.

Plataforma donde se integra la inteligencia artificial (IA) para impulsar el pensamiento complejo en estudiantes de educación superior (Sanabria-Z et al., 2023). La estrategia didáctica se basó en el enfoque de Diseño de Transición, abordando la Economía Colaborativa como desafío. El proceso de desarrollo de actividades respaldadas por IA, los retos y riesgos identificados, así como un modelo de clasificación y mejoras para futuras implementaciones, se detallan en este trabajo. Los hallazgos ofrecen una guía para equilibrar las actividades educativas potenciadas por IA y el desarrollo del pensamiento complejo en los participantes.

Las habilidades anteriores no son únicas a carreras de tecnología o ciencias de la computación, son aplicables en campos tan diversos como la economía, las finanzas y la energía. Por ello, la oportunidad de participar en actividades en línea con un fin de dominio del pensamiento computacional nos parecerá desafiante al principio, pero nos lleva a través de ejercicios interactivos, juegos o incluso desafíos que se adaptan a varios niveles de habilidad, por ende, conocimientos no solo teóricos, aquellos que con la práctica nos auxilien en la solución de problemas reales y complejos.

La plataforma debe permitir a cada estudiante aprender de manera gradual, a su propio ritmo y desde cualquier lugar con acceso a internet. En el contexto universitario y educativo en general, es crucial que cada estudiante desarrolle una mentalidad orientada a la solución de problemas y una mayor capacidad para enfrentar los desafíos del siglo XXI.

Referencia

Sanabria-Z, J., Alfaro-Ponce, B., Argüelles-Cruz, A. y Ramírez-Montoya, M. S. (2023). AI-Based Platform Design for Complex Thinking Assessment: A Case Study of an Ideathon Using the Transition Design Approach. *Computers in the Schools, 40*(4), 391–411. https://doi.org/10.1080/07380569.2023.2256711

TE INVITAMOS A REFLEXIONAR ...

¿Cómo crees que el pensamiento computacional puede influir en la forma en que abordamos y resolvemos problemas en nuestra vida diaria? ¿De qué manera piensas que están relacionados?

____

____

____

Seguramente has escuchado la frase "vivimos en un mundo digitalizado". En ese contexto, ¿cómo crees que el desarrollo de habilidades en pensamiento computacional puede ofrecerte una ventaja competitiva en el mercado laboral o en cualquier otro escenario en el que participes?

____

____

____

¿Qué beneficios crees que el pensamiento computacional puede aportar a disciplinas académicas que no están directamente relacionadas con las ciencias de la computación?

____

____

____

ODS en la Educación

Este proyecto de innovación educativa fue concebido a la luz de los Objetivos de Desarrollo Sostenible, específicamente a los ODS 3, 4, 7 y 10 (Figura 4), fundamentados en trabajar por la salud y el bienestar, una educación de calidad, fomentar las energías asequibles y no contaminantes, y reducir las desigualdades. Todo lo anterior orientado a ofrecer experiencias formativas innovadoras que ayuden a escalar el pensamiento computacional, el pensamiento complejo en la era digital y otras competencias del siglo XXI.

Figura 4. ODS movilizados a través de la plataforma de ecosistema digital E4C&CT

La plataforma E4C&CT se posiciona como un entorno abierto, que ofrece experiencias formativas innovadoras, es accesible en términos del mínimo nivel de habilidades computacionales previas, así como su disponibilidad y ergonomía digital. Además de ello, permite el desarrollo y certificación de las competencias en pensamiento computacional y está pensada para que pueda ser utilizada desde estudiantes K-12 hasta docentes, facilitadores en empresas, gobierno, fundaciones y personas interesadas en el aprendizaje a lo largo de la vida. Lo anterior permite cumplir con formar a las personas para el futuro del trabajo, a través de situaciones del mundo real siendo accesible, inclusivo y relevante para los requerimientos del mercado laboral actual.

PARA SABER MÁS...
el vínculo entre los ODS y la propuesta

Unlocking Sustainable Development Goals through Computational Thinking: A Search to Inform Computers Education from Citizen Science Dataset

Autores: María Soledad Ramírez-Montoya, Mariana Buenestado Fernández y Gerardo Ibarra Vázquez.

Referencia: Ramírez-Montoya, M. S., Buenestado-Fernandez, M. e Ibarra-Vázquez, G. (2023). Unlocking Sustainable Development Goals through Computational Thinking: A Search to Inform Computers Education from Citizen Science Dataset. En *2023 The 8th International Conference on Information and Education Innovations* (ICIEI 2023), Manchester, United Kingdom. ACM, New York, NY, USA. https://doi.org/10.1145/3594441.3594449. https://hdl.handle.net/11285/650450

▶ Te invitamos a descubrir un estudio fascinante que vincula el pensamiento complejo con el pensamiento computacional, mostrando cómo juntos pueden impulsar la resolución de problemas de alto impacto. Este estudio analizó la relación entre el pensamiento computacional y los Objetivos de Desarrollo Sostenible (ODS) utilizando técnicas de minería de textos y visualización de datos. A través de un análisis detallado de fragmentos de texto etiquetados con los ODS, se encontró que las sub-competencias del pensamiento computacional —descomposición, reconocimiento de patrones, abstracción y algoritmos— se relacionan frecuentemente con ODS clave como la educación de calidad, la igualdad de género, el agua limpia y el saneamiento, y las ciudades y comunidades sostenibles. Los resultados demuestran cómo el pensamiento computacional puede ofrecer soluciones innovadoras a problemas globales y apoyar el logro de los ODS.

Pensamiento computacional basado en realidad virtual y razonamiento complejo: caso de estudio secuencial

Autores: Carlos Enrique George-Reyes, Edgar Omar López-Caudana, María Soledad Ramírez-Montoya y Jessica Alejandra Ruiz-Ramírez.

Referencia: George-Reyes, C., López-Caudana, E. O., Ramírez-Montoya, M. S. y Ruiz-Ramírez, J. (2023). Pensamiento computacional basado en realidad virtual y razonamiento complejo: caso de estudio secuencial. *RED. Revista de Educación a Distancia 23*(73). http://dx.doi.org/10.6018/red.540841 https://hdl.handle.net/11285/650112.

▶ Para saber más te compartimos un estudio que vincula el pensamiento complejo con el pensamiento computacional, mostrando cómo se puede transformar la calidad de la educación. Se realizó una investigación con 176 estudiantes universitarios, utilizando dos herramientas para medir la aceptación del entorno virtual y el desarrollo del razonamiento complejo. Los resultados fueron sorprendentes: los estudiantes encontraron el Virtual Campus fácil de usar y útil, y la experiencia en 3D mejoró significativamente sus competencias de pensamiento científico y crítico. Este estudio demuestra que la convergencia de PC, R4C y WebVR puede crear dinámicas de aprendizaje innovadoras, alineadas con las demandas de una educación en constante evolución, y contribuir a mejorar las prácticas para la resolución de problemas.

Nuevos Escenarios Educativos

El proyecto busca dotar a los usuarios de habilidades para la resolución de problemas a través de un enfoque práctico utilizando la plataforma E4C&CT, que vincula los esfuerzos educativos con retos sociales más amplios presentados en los ODS como escenarios simulados para enseñar a resolver problemas complejos. Para ello, la plataforma plantea posibles escenarios de aplicación, que se comparten como líneas generales de actuación, que pueden adaptarse al contexto cultural, social, económico o profesional de cada usuario, fomentando el aprendizaje para la vida.

ESCENARIO EDUCATIVO dirigido a estudiantes

Aplicando el pensamiento computacional para reducir la desigualdad en el acceso a la educación

ODS vinculados

Actividad

Los participantes desarrollarán habilidades de pensamiento computacional —especialmente la descomposición— mediante el análisis del acceso desigual a la educación en su contexto local, en consonancia con el ODS 4 (Educación de calidad). A través de una fase inicial de investigación, los estudiantes identifican las principales barreras económicas, geográficas, culturales y de género, construyendo una comprensión sólida del problema. Posteriormente, aplican la descomposición creando un mapa mental que divide el problema central en subproblemas y propone al menos una solución viable para cada uno, fomentando el pensamiento crítico, sistémico y creativo. La actividad concluye con una breve reflexión sobre cómo la descomposición apoyó su comprensión y el diseño de la solución, mientras que la evaluación se realiza mediante rúbricas analíticas que valoran la identificación del problema, la profundidad del análisis, la organización y la calidad de las soluciones, siendo el mapa mental la principal evidencia del aprendizaje.

Objetivo

Analizar el problema complejo del acceso desigual a la educación mediante la aplicación de técnicas de descomposición, una subcompetencia del pensamiento computacional, para proponer soluciones aplicables a nivel local.

Inicio

El primer paso consiste en realizar una investigación inicial para identificar las causas del acceso desigual a la educación en tu comunidad local. Es crucial considerar factores como las barreras económicas, geográficas, culturales y de género. Esta etapa preliminar no solo te proporcionará una visión clara del problema, sino que también te preparará para aplicar técnicas de descomposición de manera eficiente. Asegúrate de recopilar información precisa y relevante que te permita abordar el problema de manera integral y fundamentada.

Desarrollo

Identificación del problema: realiza una investigación inicial sobre las causas del acceso desigual a la educación en tu comunidad local, identificando factores como barreras económicas, geográficas, culturales, de género, etc.

Aplicación de la técnica de descomposición

a) Construye un mapa mental para subdividir el problema.
b) Identifica en el centro la desigualdad en el acceso a la educación y ve creando ramas de las posibles causas, como, por ejemplo, la falta de infraestructura educativa en áreas rurales, la discriminación de género, la carencia de recursos educativos y materiales didácticos, la desigualdad económica en la familia de estudiantes.
c) Agrega o elimina factores con base en la situación de tu comunidad.
d) Para cada una de las ramas que identifican los subproblemas, construye subramas colocando ideas con posibles soluciones, por ejemplo, para la rama de discriminación de género en el acceso a la educación, podrías colocar el desarrollo de campañas de concientización sobre la importancia de la educación para todas las personas.
e) Agrega una posible solución a cada subproblema.

Cierre

Realiza una reflexión personal sobre el proceso de descomposición y cómo este enfoque ayudó a entender mejor el problema y a proponer soluciones factibles y aplicables en tu comunidad. Para aprender más sobre pensamiento computacional te invitamos a realizar el curso EduInnovaTech: Descomponiendo Retos para una Educación de Calidad, disponible en https://e4cct.mx/.

Evaluación

La evaluación será a través de rúbricas analíticas. La rúbrica de evaluación que proponemos ofrece un enfoque analítico para medir el desempeño en cada etapa del proceso. Está organizada en cinco criterios: identificación del problema, aplicación de la técnica de descomposición, estructura y organización del mapa mental, propuesta de soluciones, y creatividad y claridad visual. Cada criterio se valora en una escala de cuatro niveles (1 a 4), desde "Necesita mejorar" hasta "Excelente", proporcionando descripciones claras para cada nivel. Por ejemplo, en la identificación del problema, el nivel más alto se alcanza al incluir múltiples factores relevantes (económicos, culturales, de género, etc.) con ejemplos específicos de la comunidad. De manera similar, para evaluar la creatividad y claridad visual, se espera que el mapa mental no solo sea funcional, sino también atractivo, con elementos gráficos que faciliten la comprensión. Esta rúbrica permite una evaluación transparente, ayudando tanto a los participantes como a los evaluadores a comprender las expectativas.

Evidencia de Aprendizaje

Mapa mental que descompone el problema de acceso desigual a la educación en subproblemas y para cada uno de ellos se identifican al menos una posible solución.

Materiales o Herramientas Digitales

El mapa mental puede ser creado a través de herramientas tecnológicas o bien en papel.

ESCENARIO EDUCATIVO dirigido a docentes

Taller de desarrollo de competencias en pensamiento computacional y complejo para docentes

ODS vinculados

Actividad

Los participantes desarrollarán competencias de pensamiento computacional y complejo mediante el diseño de estrategias pedagógicas para abordar la desigualdad en el acceso a la educación, en consonancia con el ODS 4 (Educación de calidad). A través de un escenario real, los docentes aplicarán principios como la descomposición, el reconocimiento de patrones y el análisis de sistemas para identificar factores clave y comprender el problema en múltiples niveles. Mediante actividades colaborativas y prácticas, y herramientas como mapas conceptuales y diagramas de flujo, diseñarán soluciones adaptadas al contexto y escalables. La actividad concluye con la creación conjunta y la presentación de propuestas con retroalimentación entre pares, fomentando la reflexión crítica, la resolución colaborativa de problemas y la aplicación del pensamiento computacional a la innovación pedagógica.

Objetivo

Capacitar a docentes en el uso y aplicación de estrategias pedagógicas para desarrollar competencias de pensamiento computacional y complejo en sus estudiantes a través de un escenario de acceso a la educación para todas las personas.

Inicio

El taller inicia con una introducción al concepto de pensamiento computacional y su relevancia en la resolución de problemas complejos. Se presenta el problema del acceso desigual a la educación, destacando su impacto global y local. A través de una breve sesión teórica, cada docente aprenderá a descomponer problemas complejos en partes manejables, identificando los factores subyacentes que contribuyen a la desigualdad educativa. Este enfoque permitirá a cada participante comprender mejor las múltiples dimensiones del problema, facilitando el desarrollo de soluciones más efectivas y específicas.

Desarrollo

Durante la fase práctica, cada docente trabajará en grupos para aplicar técnicas de descomposición al problema del acceso desigual a la educación. Se les guiará para identificar y desglosar los componentes del problema, como barreras económicas, sociales y geográficas, que afectan el acceso a la educación en sus comunidades. Utilizando mapas conceptuales y diagramas de flujo, cada docente organizará y analizará la información recopilada, lo que les permitirá visualizar claramente las interrelaciones y los puntos críticos que necesitan abordarse.

Cierre

Los grupos colaborarán para generar propuestas de solución aplicables a nivel local. Estas propuestas serán discutidas y refinadas colectivamente, fomentando el intercambio de ideas y experiencias. Al concluir el taller, cada grupo presentará su análisis y las soluciones propuestas, recibiendo retroalimentación tanto de sus pares como de las personas facilitadoras.

Evaluación

La evaluación de la actividad se realizará a través de rúbricas analíticas que medirán el desempeño de cada docente en varias dimensiones, como la identificación de conceptos clave, comprensión y aplicación del pensamiento computacional, la capacidad para descomponer problemas complejos y la efectividad de las soluciones propuestas.

Evidencia de Aprendizaje

Un escenario de un problema concreto (local) sobre el acceso a la educación. Se debe contar con un diagrama de flujo y de identificación de los elementos que juegan en dicho escenario.

Materiales o Herramientas Digitales

Software de mapas conceptuales y diagramas de flujo: herramientas como Coogle, MindMeister o Lucidchart, que ayudarán a cada docente a organizar y visualizar la información de manera efectiva.

Conexión a Internet: para acceder a recursos en línea y colaborar con sus pares en tiempo real.

Proyector y pantalla: para las presentaciones teóricas y la presentación final de las propuestas de los grupos.

ESCENARIO EDUCATIVO dirigido a empresas

Taller de desarrollo de soluciones creativas para el uso de energías limpias en el sector empresarial

ODS vinculados

Actividad

Los participantes desarrollarán competencias de pensamiento computacional y complejo mediante el diseño de soluciones innovadoras de energía limpia para el sector empresarial, alineadas con el ODS 7 (Energía asequible y no contaminante). A través de un taller, los empleados aplicarán conceptos como la abstracción, la descomposición, el reconocimiento de patrones y el diseño de algoritmos a desafíos como la reducción de la huella de carbono. Utilizando herramientas de datos y el trabajo colaborativo, analizarán el consumo de energía, identificarán áreas de mejora y propondrán soluciones viables, como la integración solar o los sistemas de gestión energética. La actividad concluye con la presentación y evaluación de las propuestas, fomentando la resolución práctica de problemas, la colaboración y la aplicación del pensamiento computacional a prácticas empresariales sostenibles.

Objetivo

Capacitar a personas empleadas de empresas del sector empresarial en la identificación, desarrollo, y evaluación de soluciones creativas e innovadoras para el uso de energías limpias, utilizando herramientas y técnicas de pensamiento computacional y complejo.

Objetivos específicos

1. Fomentar la comprensión y aplicación de competencias en abstracción, descomposición, identificación de patrones y diseño de algoritmos.
2. Promover la colaboración entre empresas y estudiantes para la implementación de soluciones sostenibles.
3. Evaluar el impacto y la eficacia de las soluciones desarrolladas en el contexto empresarial.

Inicio

1. Bienvenida e introducción
   - Presentación de las personas facilitadoras y los objetivos del taller.
   - Introducción al concepto de pensamiento computacional y su importancia en la resolución de problemas complejos.
   - Presentación del problema global del cambio climático y la necesidad de soluciones energéticas limpias.
2. Presentación de la plataforma E4CCT
   - Demostración de la plataforma <https://e4cct.mx> destacando sus funciones, como videos, cuestionarios y herramientas de ciencia de datos.

Desarrollo

1. Fase teórica
   - Abstracción y descomposición
     - Introducción a las técnicas de descomposición de problemas y su aplicación en el contexto empresarial.
     - Ejemplo práctico: descomponer el problema de la alta huella de carbono en una empresa.
2. Fase práctica
   - Identificación de patrones
     - Ejercicio en grupo para identificar patrones comunes en el consumo energético de la empresa.
     - Uso de herramientas de ciencia de datos para analizar el consumo energético y detectar áreas de mejora.
   - Diseño de algoritmos
     - Desarrollo de algoritmos sencillos para optimizar el uso de energía limpia.
     - Implementación de soluciones utilizando tecnologías como paneles solares y sistemas de gestión energética.

Cierre

1. Presentación de propuestas
   - Los grupos presentarán sus análisis y soluciones propuestas.
   - Discusión y retroalimentación sobre la factibilidad y aplicabilidad de las soluciones en el contexto empresarial.
2. Evaluación y reflexión
   - Evaluación del taller mediante encuestas y rúbricas analíticas.
   - Reflexión sobre los aprendizajes adquiridos y los próximos pasos a seguir.

Evaluación

La evaluación se realizará en varias dimensiones: identificación de conceptos clave, descomposición del problema y factibilidad de las soluciones en la práctica, usando patrones y algoritmos.

Evidencia de Aprendizaje

1. Diagramas de flujo y conceptuales que muestran la descomposición del problema y las soluciones propuestas.
2. Presentación de las propuestas desarrolladas por los grupos, demostrando los patrones identificados y los algoritmos de solución.

Materiales o Herramientas Digitales

1. *Software* de mapas conceptuales y diagramas de flujo: herramientas como Coggle, MindMeister o Lucidchart para organizar y visualizar la información.
2. Conexión a Internet: para acceder a recursos en línea y colaborar en tiempo real.
3. Proyector y pantalla: para presentaciones teóricas y la presentación final de las propuestas.

ESCENARIO EDUCATIVO dirigido a ONG

Taller de desarrollo de competencias en pensamiento computacional y complejo para ONG

ODS vinculados

7 ENERGÍA ASEQUIBLE Y NO CONTAMINANTE

Actividad

Cada participante desarrollará habilidades para diseñar sistemas fotovoltaicos solares, reconocerá la importancia de energías renovables en el contexto del Objetivo de Desarrollo Sostenible 7: energía asequible y no contaminante, incidiendo en propuestas para enfrentar retos energéticos contemporáneos. Esta actividad abarca desde la selección de componentes hasta el cálculo de necesidades energéticas para aprender sobre sistemas complejos que manejan energía, fomentando el pensamiento computacional y complejo para encontrar soluciones creativas, y evidenciando la importancia de este conocimiento a lo largo de la vida y el papel de las ONG para su implementación.

Objetivo

Desarrollar la capacidad de cada participante para pensar de manera crítica y creativa sobre problemas complejos relacionados con el manejo de energía asequible y no contaminante (ODS 7), así como aprender a identificar y aplicar soluciones al problema del abastecimiento de energía sustentable a través del diseño de sistemas fotovoltaicos que pueden ser instalados en sus hogares, identificando sus componentes y calculando las necesidades energéticas.

Inicio

1. Preparación y bienvenida
   - Se configura el equipo y se asegura que los participantes cuenten con las instalaciones y el equipo necesario para la implementación, se verifica el acceso a la plataforma E4C&CT.
   - Se presenta el equipo facilitador, destacando la relevancia de la sustentabilidad energética para un abastecimiento sustentable, no solo en las empresas o negocios, sino como parte de la vida cotidiana y su utilidad en comunidades de escasos recursos o con escasez de condiciones de acceso para un desarrollo digno.
2. Introducción al curso
   - Sesión inicial sobre la importancia de las energías renovables, las opciones para fomentar la sustentabilidad energética y el papel de la sociedad civil y las organizaciones no gubernamentales en la educación a lo largo de la vida sobre el tema energético.
3. Presentación del caso de estudio
   - Se les presenta a los participantes, en primer lugar, los componentes de un sistema fotovoltaico y la forma de calcular los consumos energéticos de cada uno de ellos, realizando algunos ejercicios.
   - Se les presenta a los participantes un estudio de caso en una comunidad rural con requisitos modestos de consumo de energía, principalmente en iluminación, refrigeración y ventilación, pero con acceso limitado a electricidad por infraestructura, por lo que dependen en gran medida de los combustibles fósiles, que son costosos y dañinos para el medio ambiente. Los participantes deben descomponer este problema e ir calculando los consumos energéticos para lograr proponer una solución de uso de energía mediante una fotocelda.

Desarrollo

1. Ingresar a la plataforma E4C&CT.
2. Leer el caso de estudio.
3. Las personas participantes trabajarán en grupos para proponer soluciones innovadoras a problemas relacionados con la energía sostenible, fomentando la colaboración y el desarrollo de habilidades blandas.
4. Análisis de las soluciones encontradas, las estrategias implementadas por cada equipo, y reflexionar sobre los aprendizajes clave y la importancia de las ONG para fomentar la gestión y aprovechamiento de recursos energéticos renovables y sustentables.

Cierre

Cada equipo hará un comentario sobre su experiencia al usar el pensamiento computacional para encontrar soluciones a problemas complejos, reflexionarán sobre sus logros individuales y grupales durante el taller, finalmente explicarán qué opciones de implementación les parecen viables como ONG.

Evaluación

A partir del estudio de caso presentado en la plataforma, se solicita a cada participante de una ONG incorporarse a un equipo y desarrollar una solución al caso, por lo que los aprendizajes clave adquiridos y sus opiniones al respecto quedan registradas en la plataforma mediante instrumentos que evalúan el contenido técnico y la usabilidad de la plataforma.

Se utilizarán pruebas que están incorporadas en la plataforma antes y después de la actividad para medir el aprendizaje, encuestas de satisfacción, y propuestas de solución a un estudio de caso desarrollado por cada participante. Instrumentos incorporados en plataforma: eComplexity (Castillo-Martínez y Ramírez-Montoya, 2022) y User experience.

Evidencia de aprendizaje: cada participante realiza los cuestionarios que evalúan conocimientos técnicos, una evidencia de solución del caso mediante un archivo que deben subir a la plataforma, y las actividades del foro y de co-creación alusivas al tema de energía sustentable y diseño de sistemas fotovoltaicos.

Evidencia de Aprendizaje

1. Diagramas de flujo y conceptuales que muestran la descomposición del problema y las soluciones propuestas.
2. Presentación de las propuestas desarrolladas por los grupos, demostrando los patrones identificados y los algoritmos de solución.

Materiales o Herramientas Digitales

- Acceso a la plataforma E4C&CT y recursos educativos complementarios.
- Videos, infografías y guías prácticas para facilitar el aprendizaje continuo y autónomo.
- Materiales de apoyo y documentación para reforzar conceptos aprendidos durante el curso.

Referencia

Castillo-Martínez, I. M. y Ramírez-Montoya, M. S. (2022). Instrumento eComplexity: Medición de la percepción de estudiantes de educación superior acerca de su competencia de razonamiento para la complejidad. https://hdl.handle.net/11285/643622

ESCENARIO EDUCATIVO dirigido a *life long learning*

Taller de desarrollo de competencias en Pensamiento Computacional y Complejo para el aprendizaje a lo largo de la vida

ODS vinculados

7 ENERGÍA ASEQUIBLE Y NO CONTAMINANTE

Actividad

Cada participante reconocerá la importancia de las energías renovables en el contexto del objetivo de desarrollo sostenible 7: energía asequible y no contaminante, incidiendo en propuestas para enfrentar retos energéticos contemporáneos a partir de su propia experiencia de vida. Esta actividad desarrollará habilidades para diseñar sistemas fotovoltaicos solares, desde la selección de componentes hasta el cálculo de necesidades energéticas, fomentando el pensamiento computacional y complejo, para enfrentar los desafíos de un futuro cada día más complejo.

Objetivo

Desarrollar la capacidad de cada participante para que, a partir de su experiencia de vida, aborde de manera crítica y creativa problemas complejos sobre abastecimiento de energía sustentable a través del diseño de sistemas fotovoltaicos que pueden ser instalados en hogares, identificando sus componentes y calculando las necesidades energéticas.

Inicio

Se motiva a los participantes con un video alusivo al ODS7, se les solicita expresar situaciones que hayan vivido o sean cercanas a lo presenciado en el video y se les presenta al equipo facilitador quien destaca la relevancia de la sustentabilidad energética para un abastecimiento sustentable como parte de la vida cotidiana.

Posteriormente, se los apoya para su ingreso a la plataforma E4C&CT, se les presentan las opciones para fomentar la sustentabilidad energética, los componentes de un sistema fotovoltaico y la forma de calcular los consumos energéticos de cada uno de ellos, realizando algunos ejercicios. Las personas participantes trabajarán en grupos, fomentando la colaboración y el desarrollo de habilidades blandas.

Desarrollo

Se les presenta a los participantes un estudio de caso en una comunidad rural con requisitos modestos de consumo de energía (iluminación, refrigeración y ventilación), sin acceso a electricidad, dependientes de combustibles fósiles, costosos y dañinos para el medio ambiente. Los participantes deben descomponer este problema e ir calculando los consumos energéticos para lograr proponer una solución de uso de energía mediante una fotocelda.

Cierre

Cada equipo presentará su solución para discusión grupal, hará un comentario sobre su experiencia al usar el pensamiento computacional para encontrar soluciones a problemas complejos, reflexionarán sobre sus logros individuales y grupales durante el curso, y la importancia de la gestión y aprovechamiento de recursos energéticos renovables y sustentables como parte de los retos que preparan a las personas para los desafíos del futuro.

Evaluación

Se utilizarán pruebas que están incorporadas en la plataforma antes y después de la actividad para medir el aprendizaje, encuestas de satisfacción, y propuestas de solución a un estudio de caso desarrollado por cada equipo.

Instrumentos incorporados en plataforma: eComplexity (Castillo-Martínez y Ramírez-Montoya, 2022) y User experience.

Evidencia de Aprendizaje

Mediante actividades en el foro, ejercicios de co-creación y cuestionarios, cada participante evalúa sus conocimientos técnicos y comparte su evidencia de solución del caso de diseño de sistemas fotovoltaicos, todo a través de la plataforma.

Materiales o Herramientas Digitales

Acceso a la plataforma E4C&CT y los recursos complementarios que aloja como videos, infografías y guías prácticas para facilitar el aprendizaje continuo y autónomo.

Referencia

Castillo-Martínez, I. M. y Ramírez-Montoya, M. S. (2022). Instrumento eComplexity: Medición de la percepción de estudiantes de educación superior acerca de su competencia de razonamiento para la complejidad. https://hdl.handle.net/11285/643622

Recomendaciones para la Implementación

Para realizar una implementación se recomienda seguir el siguiente plan de trabajo (Figura 5).

Preparación

- Antes de la implementación, asegúrate de que todas las personas facilitadoras y participantes se familiaricen con la plataforma. Realiza sesiones de capacitación preliminares si es necesario.

- Realiza pruebas técnicas para asegurarte que todos los equipos y conexiones a internet funcionen correctamente. Verifica que todos los enlaces y accesos estén operativos.

- Asegúrate de que cada participante tenga su cuenta creada y configurada correctamente. Proporciona instrucciones claras sobre cómo iniciar sesión y navegar por la plataforma

Durante la implementación

- Utiliza todas las funcionalidades disponibles en la plataforma, como videos, cuestionarios, instrumentos de encuesta y herramientas de ciencia de datos, para ofrecer una experiencia completa y enriquecedora.

- Fomenta la interacción y la colaboración entre las personas participantes mediante foros de discusión, chats en vivo y trabajos en grupo. Esto ayudará a crear un entorno de aprendizaje dinámico y participativo.

- Monitorea el progreso de cada participante regularmente. Utiliza las herramientas de análisis y seguimiento de la plataforma para identificar áreas donde las personas participantes puedan necesitar apoyo adicional.

Post-implementación

- Realiza un análisis exhaustivo de los datos recopilados durante la implementación. Utiliza estos datos para evaluar la efectividad de la plataforma y el impacto en las habilidades de resolución de problemas computacionales de cada participante.

- Identifica áreas de mejora basadas en la retroalimentación y el análisis de datos. Actualiza y mejora continuamente la plataforma y los materiales de capacitación para futuras implementaciones.

- Comparte los resultados y aprendizajes con todos los stakeholders involucrados. Difunde los éxitos y las mejores prácticas a través de informes, publicaciones y presentaciones.

Figura 5. Recomendaciones para implementar la plataforma de ecosistema digital E4C&CT

Aplicaciones en el mundo real

La plataforma E4C&CT se distingue por hacer **énfasis en la aplicación de habilidades de** pensamiento computacional y pensamiento complejo a retos del mundo real, proporcionando a los alumnos experiencias prácticas que van más allá de los conocimientos teóricos. A través del aprendizaje basado en escenarios, los participantes se involucran en tareas modeladas a partir de situaciones del mundo real, como el análisis del consumo de energía. Cada escenario refleja las complejidades de estos problemas globales, a menudo enmarcados por los Objetivos de Desarrollo Sostenible (ODS).

Por ejemplo, los alumnos pueden trabajar en un proyecto relacionado con el ODS 7, en el que utilizan el pensamiento computacional para desarrollar soluciones de eficiencia energética con diseño de energías renovables para una comunidad con acceso limitado a la electricidad.

En este escenario, los participantes analizarían los patrones de consumo de energía, descompondrían el problema en componentes manejables y diseñarían algoritmos para optimizar el uso de la energía. Estas tareas prácticas simulan los procesos de toma de decisiones requeridos en entornos profesionales, proporcionando a los participantes valiosas perspectivas sobre cómo el pensamiento computacional y complejo puede impulsar soluciones innovadoras.

Al aplicar sus habilidades en estos contextos reales, los alumnos desarrollan competencias críticas en resolución de problemas, análisis de datos y pensamiento sistémico. La plataforma también integra herramientas de inteligencia artificial y análisis de datos para proporcionar información en tiempo real, lo que permite a los alumnos perfeccionar sus enfoques. Este enfoque práctico prepara a los usuarios para afrontar retos en diversos sectores, como la educación, la tecnología y la energía, lo que convierte a la plataforma E4C&CT en un recurso muy valioso para formar profesionales preparados para el futuro, capaces de abordar los problemas más apremiantes del mundo.

Impacto en la alfabetización digital

La plataforma E4C&CT desempeña un papel fundamental en la mejora de la alfabetización digital al dotar a los alumnos de las competencias esenciales del siglo XXI necesarias para triunfar en un mundo cada vez más impulsado por la tecnología. A través de su enfoque de aprendizaje interactivo basado en escenarios, la plataforma cultiva una profunda comprensión de las competencias digitales básicas, como el análisis de datos, la resolución de problemas y el pensamiento algorítmico. Los participantes no solo aprenden a utilizar las herramientas digitales, sino que también desarrollan la capacidad de evaluar críticamente y aplicar estas herramientas para abordar problemas complejos del mundo real. La integración de la inteligencia artificial y la ciencia de datos refuerza aún más su capacidad para gestionar, interpretar y utilizar eficazmente la información digital. Este enfoque holístico de la alfabetización digital va más allá de la competencia tecnológica básica, capacitando a los alumnos para ser adaptables e innovadores ante la evolución de los entornos digitales y las exigencias profesionales. Al participar en la plataforma E4C&CT, los usuarios adquieren las habilidades necesarias para navegar, contribuir y liderar dentro de una fuerza de trabajo global en rápida digitalización.

Estrategias de inclusión

El Ecosistema Digital E4C&CT avanza a pasos agigantados en la promoción de la inclusión aprovechando el poder de las herramientas avanzadas de accesibilidad, en particular UserWay Toolbox. UserWay es un proveedor de soluciones de accesibilidad digital que mejora la accesibilidad de las plataformas digitales incorporando funciones basadas en la inteligencia artificial. Esta caja de herramientas desempeña un papel fundamental a la hora de derribar barreras como la brecha digital, y garantizar que la plataforma llegue a comunidades desatendidas o marginadas, en particular a aquellas con discapacidades o acceso limitado a la tecnología.

Como se muestra en la Figura 6, UserWay Toolbox ofrece una variedad de funcionalidades para satisfacer las necesidades de personas con diferentes necesidades de accesibilidad. Estas funciones contribuyen a fomentar la inclusión al abordar diversas discapacidades, como limitaciones motoras, visuales, cognitivas y auditivas. Algunas de las características clave de la caja de herramientas son:

- **Accesibilidad para discapacitados motores.** Esta característica mejora la usabilidad de la plataforma para las personas que pueden tener dificultades para utilizar un ratón o un teclado estándar. La caja de herramientas incluye opciones como cursores más grandes, ayuda a la navegación con el teclado y funcionalidad de comandos de voz. Esto garantiza que las personas con discapacidades motrices puedan navegar por la plataforma sin esfuerzo e interactuar con su contenido.
- **Integración del lector de pantalla.** Para los usuarios con discapacidad visual, la funcionalidad de lector de pantalla lee en voz alta el texto que aparece en la pantalla, lo que permite a los usuarios acceder al contenido sin depender de la vista. Esta integración garantiza que los usuarios ciegos o con baja visión puedan interactuar con la plataforma sin obstáculos.

- **Personalización del texto.** Funciones como el texto más grande, el ajuste del contraste y el espaciado del texto permiten a los usuarios con discapacidades cognitivas o visuales ajustar la visualización del texto a sus necesidades. Para los usuarios con dislexia, el modo adaptado a la dislexia optimiza la visualización del texto para facilitar la lectura cambiando el estilo y el diseño de la fuente para mejorar la legibilidad.
- **Asistencia para daltónicos.** Los usuarios con daltonismo pueden beneficiarse de la configuración de ajuste de color, asegurando que el contenido visual sea accesible para individuos con varios tipos de daltonismo, garantizando así una experiencia visual inclusiva.
- **Consideraciones sobre convulsiones y epilepsia.** Para las personas sensibles a las luces parpadeantes o animaciones, la función pausar animaciones garantiza una experiencia de navegación segura al detener el contenido dinámico que podría desencadenar convulsiones.
- **TDAH y ayuda a la atención.** Los usuarios con condiciones relacionadas con la atención pueden beneficiarse de características tales como el aumento de espaciado de texto y herramientas de mejora de enfoque, que ayudan a mantener la concentración y el interés por el contenido de la plataforma.
- **Acceso multilingüe y multimodal.** La plataforma admite varios idiomas, como indica el selector de idiomas de UserWay Toolbox, lo que permite a usuarios de diversos orígenes lingüísticos acceder a la plataforma en su idioma preferido. Esto amplía el alcance de la plataforma a comunidades de todo el mundo, especialmente en regiones donde el inglés puede no ser la primera lengua.

Al incorporar UserWay Toolbox a la plataforma E4C&CT, abordamos no solo las barreras físicas y cognitivas, sino también las creadas por la brecha digital. Estas funciones garantizan que los usuarios de diversas comunidades marginadas —como las personas con discapacidad o que viven en regiones con acceso limitado a recursos educativos— puedan participar plenamente en la plataforma y beneficiarse de sus contenidos educativos. Esta integración apoya el objetivo general de la inclusión, en consonancia con los objetivos de desarrollo sostenible (ODS), promoviendo el acceso equitativo a una educación de calidad.

En resumen, UserWay Toolbox garantiza que la plataforma E4C&CT sea accesible a una amplia gama de usuarios, lo que permite que el ecosistema proporcione experiencias educativas significativas a todos, independientemente de sus limitaciones físicas, cognitivas o lingüísticas. Estas estrategias de inclusión posicionan a la plataforma para derribar barreras y ofrecer un entorno de aprendizaje accesible y equitativo para todos los usuarios.

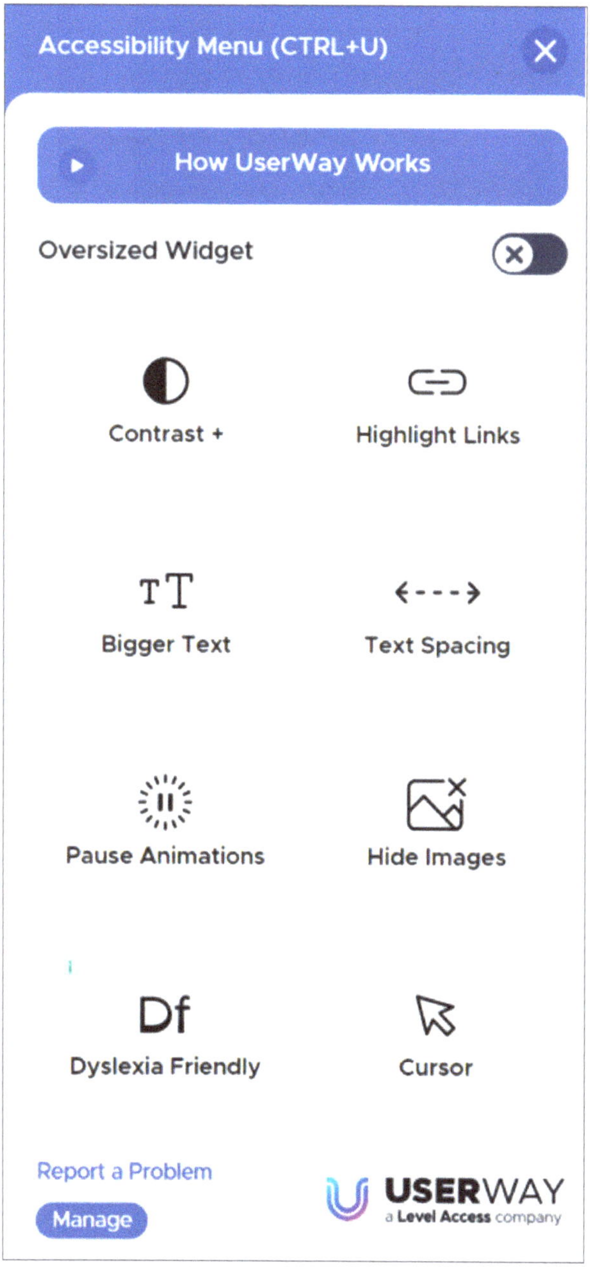

Figura 6. Integración de UserWay en E4C&CT

RECURSOS EDUCATIVOS ABIERTOS (REA)

REA: The E4CCT Ecosystem: An open educational ecosystem for collaboration and training.
Autora: Irma Azeneth Patiño Zúñiga.
Referencia: Patiño Zúñiga, I. A. (2024). *The E4CCT Ecosystem: An open educational ecosystem for collaboration and training* [Video]. https://hdl.handle.net/11285/676170

▶ Te compartimos un recurso educativo, en formato video, que te llevará a un viaje fascinante a través de un ecosistema digital diseñado para desarrollar habilidades de pensamiento computacional y razonamiento complejo. Imagina que estamos viendo juntos este video, que nos ofrece una visión general del proyecto E4CCT, incluyendo sus objetivos, metodología y el impacto transformador que ha tenido en la educación. A lo largo del video, aprenderemos cómo estas herramientas de aprendizaje personalizadas, adaptadas a las capacidades individuales de cada estudiante, promueven habilidades críticas y de pensamiento complejo, mejorando significativamente la calidad educativa. Únete a esta experiencia y descubramos juntos cómo podemos impulsar el aprendizaje y preparar a los estudiantes para los desafíos del futuro. ¡Vamos a co-construir!

REA: STEM Roadmap for Mobilizing Open Education.
Autores: María Soledad Ramírez-Montoya, Carolina Alcantar Nieblas y José Vladimir Burgos Aguilar.
Referencia: Ramírez-Montoya, M. S., Alcantar Nieblas, C. y Burgos Aguilar, J. V. (2024). *STEM Roadmap for Mobilizing Open Education* [Video]. https://hdl.handle.net/11285/676163

▶ Te invitamos a unirte en una experiencia única a través de un recurso educativo, en formato video, que presenta una fascinante Hoja de Ruta STEM para Movilizar la Educación Abierta, y nos guía a través del emocionante proceso de postulación al programa STEM Roadmap 2024. Imagínate que estamos explorando juntos los detalles del programa, sus objetivos y los pasos necesarios para participar. A través de este recurso, entenderemos cómo esta iniciativa puede transformar nuestras oportunidades educativas y abrir nuevas puertas en el mundo de la ciencia, la tecnología, la ingeniería y las matemáticas. Acompáñanos en esta aventura de aprendizaje y descubramos juntos cómo podemos ser parte de este innovador programa. ¡Vamos a construir en red!

REA: Programando el futuro: cuartos de escape digital.
Autores: José Martín Molina Espinosa y Paloma Suárez Brito.
Referencia: Molina Espinosa, J. M. y Suárez- Brito, P. (2023). Programando el futuro: cuartos de escape digital [Video]. *Programa de webcast: Futuro de la educación en la complejidad.* Tecnológico de Monterrey. https://repositorio.tec.mx/handle/11285/651632

▶ Compartimos un recurso educativo, en formato video, que comparte la emocionante experiencia de utilizar escape digital en la educación superior para evaluar competencias de pensamiento computacional y complejo. Imagina que estamos sentados juntos, escuchando a Paloma Suárez y Martín Molina en un panel inspirador, donde nos cuentan cómo estas dinámicas de escape digital pueden transformar nuestras metodologías de enseñanza. A través de este recurso, descubriremos cómo estas herramientas interactivas no solo hacen que el aprendizaje sea más divertido, sino también cómo pueden medir de manera efectiva habilidades cruciales en nuestros estudiantes. Únete a esta comunidad de aprendizaje y descubramos juntos nuevas formas de enseñar y evaluar. ¡Vamos a aprender juntos!

REA: Rompiendo códigos y construyendo habilidades de pensamiento computacional.
Autores: Román Martínez y Amadeo Argüelles.
Referencia: Martínez, R. y Argüelles, A. (2023). Rompiendo códigos y construyendo habilidades de pensamiento computacional [Video]. *Programa de webcast: Futuro de la educación en la complejidad.* Tecnológico de Monterrey. https://hdl.handle.net/11285/676176

▶ Te invitamos a un fascinante viaje a través de un recurso educativo en video que no puedes perderte. Este video, titulado "Rompiendo códigos y construyendo habilidades de pensamiento computacional" nos presenta una innovadora plataforma tecnológica diseñada para estudiantes de educación superior. Imagínate que estamos juntos en un panel con Román Mendoza y Amadeo Argüelles, quienes nos explican detalladamente qué es esta herramienta, cómo funciona y para qué se utiliza. A lo largo del video, entenderemos la importancia del pensamiento computacional en el ámbito empresarial y cómo esta plataforma puede equipar a los estudiantes con habilidades esenciales para el futuro. Acompáñanos en esta emocionante exploración y descubramos juntos cómo podemos aprovechar esta tecnología para mejorar nuestra educación y preparación profesional. ¡Vamos a crecer en comunidad!

REA: Detecting Generative Artificial Intelligence Essays using Large Language Models: Machine and Deep Learning Approaches.
Autores: Rasikh Tariq, Fidel Antonio Guadalupe Casillas-Muñoz, Muhammad Ashraf Waqar y María Soledad Ramírez-Montoya.
Referencia: Tariq, R., Casillas-Muñoz, F., Ashraf, W. M. y Ramírez-Montoya, M. S. (2024). Detecting Generative Artificial Intelligence Essays using Large Language Models: Machine and Deep Learning Approaches [Texto]. En *2024 International Conference on Engineering & Computing Technologies* (ICECT) (pp. 1-6). IEEE. Handle: https://hdl.handle.net/11285/675892

▶ Hoy queremos invitarte a explorar un recurso educativo, en formato texto, que aborda un tema fascinante y muy relevante: cómo detectar ensayos generados por inteligencia artificial usando modelos avanzados de aprendizaje automático y profundo. Imagina que estamos juntos desentrañando los secretos de este estudio, que se centra en distinguir entre ensayos escritos por humanos y aquellos generados por IA, resaltando las implicaciones éticas en el ámbito académico. Aquí analizaremos cómo se emplean algoritmos como la regresión logística, SVM (Máquina de Vectores de Soporte), árboles de decisión, bosques aleatorios, KNN y LSTM para desarrollar modelos que clasifiquen ensayos. Aprenderás sobre la técnica TF-IDF, que evalúa la importancia de las palabras en un documento, y cómo se afinan los parámetros para garantizar la precisión del modelo. Los hallazgos destacan la precisión y capacidad de SVM para clasificar ensayos con precisión, mientras que los árboles de decisión, aunque sencillos, presentan un mayor riesgo de clasificación errónea. KNN y los bosques aleatorios ofrecen un buen equilibrio, y LSTM sobresale en la comprensión contextual, aunque requiere más recursos computacionales. Este estudio subraya la importancia de seleccionar el algoritmo adecuado para mantener la integridad académica y fomentar la creatividad genuina de los estudiantes. ¡Acompáñanos en esta aventura de aprendizaje y descubramos juntos nuevos aprendizajes!

Conclusión

En una era en la que los retos globales son cada vez más complejos e interconectados, el desarrollo de habilidades de pensamiento computacional y complejo es esencial. La plataforma del ecosistema digital E4C&CT surge como una herramienta educativa transformadora diseñada para reducir la brecha entre el conocimiento teórico y la aplicación práctica. Al integrar el aprendizaje basado en escenarios alineados con los Objetivos de Desarrollo Sostenible (ODS), la plataforma dota a los alumnos de las competencias necesarias para navegar y abordar eficazmente los problemas del mundo real.

A lo largo de esta guía, hemos explorado cómo la plataforma E4C&CT fomenta un enfoque interdisciplinar, vinculando el pensamiento computacional con el razonamiento complejo para proporcionar una experiencia de aprendizaje holística. La incorporación exclusiva de tecnologías avanzadas, como la inteligencia artificial y la ciencia de datos, no solo mejora la alfabetización digital, sino que también personaliza el viaje de aprendizaje de cada participante. Esto garantiza que alumnos de diversos orígenes puedan acceder, participar y beneficiarse de la plataforma, promoviendo la inclusión y la equidad en la educación.

La plataforma E4C&CT representa un avance significativo en la innovación educativa, al reducir la brecha entre el conocimiento teórico y la aplicación práctica de las habilidades de pensamiento computacional y de pensamiento complejo. Al sumergir a los alumnos en escenarios del mundo real alineados con los Objetivos de Desarrollo Sostenible, los prepara para abordar con eficacia las complejidades de los desafíos globales modernos. La integración única en la plataforma de tecnologías avanzadas, como la inteligencia artificial y la ciencia de datos, refuerza la alfabetización digital, fomentando las competencias esenciales del siglo XXI.

Entre las repercusiones previstas a largo plazo figuran la transformación de las prácticas educativas, la influencia en el desarrollo de políticas y la capacitación de una generación diversa de personas capaces de resolver problemas e impulsar el desarrollo sostenible en todo el mundo. Al ofrecer un ecosistema de aprendizaje inclusivo y accesible, la plataforma E4C&CT tiene el potencial de tener un impacto duradero y positivo tanto en las personas como en la sociedad, dando forma a un futuro en el que el pensamiento innovador conduzca a un cambio significativo.

LLAMADO A LA ACCIÓN

¿Te gustaría participar en el proyecto?
¡Bienvenido al emocionante proyecto de diseño y evaluación de un ecosistema digital de última generación!

Permítenos presentarte una oportunidad única para mejorar tus habilidades de resolución de problemas a partir de fomentar el pensamiento computacional. Por favor comunícate con nosotros a través de la plataforma <https://e4cct.mx> para sugerencias y opciones de colaboración para generar una herramienta de vanguardia que incluye la inteligencia artificial, el aprendizaje automático y la ciencia de datos.

Imagina tener acceso a un ecosistema digital en el que puedas diagnosticar, desarrollar y evaluar tus habilidades de pensamiento complejo, no solo para enfrentar tus estudios, sino para enfrentarte a los desafíos a lo largo de la vida, todo en un solo lugar. Ya sea que seas estudiante universitario, una persona profesional en busca de mejorar su capacidad de pensamiento complejo o simplemente alguien con interés en potenciar sus habilidades en este campo, ¡tenemos algo increíble para ti! No pierdas la oportunidad de formar parte de este emocionante proyecto. Únete a nosotros y sé parte de la revolución de la educación, a través de este ecosistema digital.

¡De manera colaborativa haremos que tus habilidades alcancen nuevas alturas!
Nuestro grupo de investigación: https://tec.mx/es/r4c-irg
Explora nuestros proyectos: https://www.research4challenges.world/

Únete al proyecto Ecosistema digital E4C&CT:
https://www.research4challenges.world/computationalthink

GLOSARIO

Descomposición. Es uno de los pilares del pensamiento computacional y consiste en descomponer un problema complejo en componentes más pequeños y manejables.

Pensamiento computacional. Proceso de resolución de problemas que implica descomponer un problema grande en partes más pequeñas y manejables, identificar patrones, abstraer detalles irrelevantes y diseñar algoritmos (una serie de pasos) para encontrar soluciones eficientes. Es una habilidad fundamental en informática y se puede aplicar en muchas áreas más allá de la programación. Por ejemplo, imagina que necesitas organizar una fiesta. Primero, divides la tarea en partes más pequeñas: elegir una fecha, hacer una lista de invitados, planificar el menú, y decorar el espacio. Luego, identificas patrones de fiestas anteriores que fueron exitosas, como qué tipo de comida y música prefirieron los invitados. A continuación, abstraes los detalles irrelevantes, como considerar solo los invitados que viven cerca. Finalmente, creas un plan paso a paso para llevar a cabo cada tarea, asegurándote de que todo esté listo a tiempo. Este proceso refleja la manera en que un programador abordaría un problema complejo usando el pensamiento computacional.

Pensamiento complejo. Es la capacidad de entender y gestionar problemas o situaciones que tienen múltiples componentes interrelacionados y que no tienen una solución única o simple. Involucra considerar diferentes perspectivas, reconocer conexiones entre distintos elementos y anticipar las consecuencias de diferentes acciones. Por ejemplo, imagina que estás gestionando un proyecto para reducir la contaminación en una ciudad. Esto no solo implica identificar las fuentes de contaminación (como fábricas y tráfico), sino también entender cómo las medidas propuestas (como regular las emisiones industriales o fomentar el uso de bicicletas) afectarán a la economía, la salud pública y la vida cotidiana de las personas. Tendrás que considerar las opiniones de distintos grupos (ciudadanos, empresas, gobierno) y encontrar un equilibrio que minimice la contaminación sin causar otros problemas graves. Esta capacidad para navegar y resolver situaciones complejas es la esencia del pensamiento complejo.

Recurso Educativo Abierto (REA). Materiales didácticos, de aprendizaje o investigación que se encuentran en dominio público o que se publican con licencias de propiedad intelectual que facilitan su uso, adaptación y distribución gratuitos.

Tecnologías 5.0. Tecnologías emergentes asociadas a la quinta revolución industrial, que hacen hincapié en la colaboración entre humanos y máquinas, incluyendo IA avanzada, robótica y análisis de datos.

Abstracción. El proceso de reducir la complejidad centrándose en la idea principal e ignorando detalles específicos, lo que hace que los problemas sean más fáciles de entender y resolver.

Algoritmo. Conjunto de instrucciones paso a paso diseñadas para realizar una tarea específica o resolver un problema de manera eficiente.

Pensamiento algorítmico. La capacidad de crear una serie de pasos ordenados para resolver un problema o realizar una tarea, fundamental para el pensamiento computacional.

Inteligencia artificial (IA). La simulación de procesos de inteligencia humana por parte de máquinas, lo que les permite realizar tareas que normalmente requieren inteligencia humana, como el aprendizaje y la resolución de problemas.

Análisis de datos. La ciencia que analiza los datos en bruto para extraer conclusiones significativas y fundamentar la toma de decisiones.

Minería de datos. El proceso de descubrir patrones y relaciones en grandes conjuntos de datos para extraer información valiosa.

Ciencia de datos. Un campo interdisciplinar que combina la estadística, la informática y la experiencia en el sector para extraer conocimientos e ideas de los datos.

Árboles de decisión. Modelo similar a un diagrama de flujo utilizado en la toma de decisiones y el aprendizaje automático que traza los posibles resultados de una serie de elecciones relacionadas.

Descomposición. Una habilidad fundamental del pensamiento computacional que consiste en dividir problemas complejos en partes más pequeñas y manejables.

Aprendizaje profundo. Un subconjunto del aprendizaje automático que implica redes neuronales con muchas capas que pueden aprender patrones complejos en grandes cantidades de datos.

Alfabetización digital. La capacidad de utilizar eficazmente las herramientas y tecnologías digitales para encontrar, evaluar, crear y comunicar información.

Minería de datos educativos. La práctica de analizar datos de entornos educativos para mejorar los resultados del aprendizaje y comprender el comportamiento de los estudiantes.

Intervenciones educativas. Estrategias o programas implementados para mejorar los resultados educativos o abordar desafíos específicos de aprendizaje.

Educación equitativa. La educación que es justa e inclusiva, proporcionando igualdad de oportunidades de aprendizaje independientemente de los antecedentes o capacidades de los estudiantes.

Gamificación. La aplicación de elementos de diseño de juegos en contextos no lúdicos para involucrar y motivar a las personas a alcanzar sus objetivos.

Educación inclusiva. Enfoque educativo en el que todos los alumnos, independientemente de sus capacidades o discapacidades, aprenden juntos en la misma aula adaptada a su edad.

K-Nearest Neighbors (KNN). Un algoritmo sencillo de aprendizaje automático utilizado para la clasificación y la regresión mediante el análisis de los «k» puntos de datos más cercanos.

Análisis del aprendizaje. La recopilación y el análisis de datos sobre los alumnos para mejorar la calidad de la educación y personalizar las experiencias de aprendizaje.

Regresión logística. Método estadístico para analizar conjuntos de datos en los que hay una o más variables independientes que determinan un resultado, utilizado para tareas de clasificación binaria.

Memoria larga a corto plazo (LSTM): Tipo de arquitectura de red neuronal capaz de aprender la dependencia del orden en problemas de predicción de secuencias.

Aprendizaje automático. Un subconjunto de la IA que permite a los ordenadores aprender de los datos y mejorar su rendimiento con el tiempo sin ser programados explícitamente.

Microcertificado. Una credencial que representa la realización de un curso corto o un conjunto de habilidades específicas, a menudo apilable hacia una cualificación mayor.

Reconocimiento de patrones. Identificación y análisis de patrones o regularidades en los datos, esencial para predecir futuras tendencias de los datos.

Filogenética. Estudio de las relaciones evolutivas entre entidades biológicas, a menudo representadas mediante un "árbol genealógico" de especies.

Bosques aleatorios. Técnica de aprendizaje automático que construye múltiples árboles de decisión y los fusiona para obtener una predicción más precisa y estable.

Aprendizaje basado en escenarios. Un enfoque de diseño instruccional que utiliza escenarios interactivos para apoyar el aprendizaje activo y aplicar los conocimientos en contextos del mundo real.

Máquina de vectores soporte (SVM). Algoritmo de aprendizaje automático supervisado que se utiliza para tareas de clasificación y regresión mediante la búsqueda del mejor límite que separa las clases.

Objetivos de Desarrollo Sostenible (ODS). Conjunto de 17 objetivos globales establecidos por las Naciones Unidas para abordar retos apremiantes como la pobreza, la desigualdad y el cambio climático para 2030.

Frecuencia de términos-Frecuencia inversa de documentos (TF-IDF): Estadística numérica utilizada para reflejar la importancia de una palabra en un documento de una colección, comúnmente utilizada en minería de textos.

Minería de textos. Proceso de obtención de información significativa a partir de un texto en lenguaje natural, que suele implicar un análisis computacional para identificar patrones.

Enfoque de diseño de transición. Un marco para abordar problemas sociales complejos previendo y facilitando el cambio sistémico a lo largo del tiempo.

Realidad virtual (RV). Simulación generada por ordenador de un entorno tridimensional con el que se puede interactuar mediante equipos electrónicos especiales.

WebVR. Un estándar abierto que permite experiencias de realidad virtual dentro de un navegador web, haciendo accesible la RV sin aplicaciones especializadas.

Competencias del siglo XXI. Habilidades esenciales para el éxito en el mundo actual, incluyendo el pensamiento crítico, la creatividad, la colaboración, la comunicación y la alfabetización digital.

Futuro de la Educación – Future of Education

Edited by María Soledad Ramírez-Montoya, Rasikh Tariq, Leonardo David Glasserman Morales, Edgar Omar López-Caudana & Inés Alvarez-Icaza Longoria

VOL. 1 María Soledad Ramírez-Montoya, Edgar Omar López-Caudana, Inés Alvarez-Icaza Longoria, Carlos Vásquez-Parra, Fabian Eduardo Basabe, Carolina Alcántar-Nieblas, Pamela Geraldine Olivo Montaño, Virginia Rodés Paragarino, Isolda Margarita Castillo-Martínez, Laura Icela González-Pérez & May Portuguez Castro: Mobilise Your Thinking for Complexity. Open Educational Model for Complex Thinking – Moviliza tu Pensamiento para la Complejidad. Modelo Educativo Abierto para el Pensamiento Complejo. 2026.

VOL. 2 María Soledad Ramírez-Montoya, Edgar Omar López-Caudana, Inés Alvarez-Icaza Longoria, Carlos Enrique George-Reyes, Paloma Suárez Brito & Pamela Geraldine Olivo Montaño: Education 5.0 to mobilise social, scientific and technological entrepreneurship. OpenEdR4C Platform – Educación 5.0 para movilizar emprendimiento social, científico y tecnológico. Plataforma OpenEdR4C. 2026.

VOL. 3 María Soledad Ramírez-Montoya, Rasikh Tariq, Edgar Omar López-Caudana, José Martín Molina Espinosa, Miguel González Mendoza, Carlos Enrique George-Reyes, Magally Martínez Reyes, Irma Azeneth Patiño Zúñiga, Fidel Antonio Guadalupe Casillas-Múñoz, Hugo Alexander Rozo-García, Paloma Suárez Brito & Pamela Geraldine Olivo Montaño: Boost Your Computational and Complex Thinking. E4C&CT Digital Ecosystem Platform – Impulsa tu Pensamiento Computacional y Razonamiento Complejo. Plataforma de Ecosistema Digital E4C&CT. 2026.

www.peterlang.com

Printed by
CPI books GmbH, Leck